OWEN SOUND

OWEN SOUND

The Port City

Paul White

NATURAL HERITAGE BOOKS
TORONTO

Published by Natural Heritage/Natural History Inc.
P.O. Box 95, Station O, Toronto, Ontario M4A 2M8

Edited by Jane Gibson
Design by Blanche Hamill, Norton Hamill Design
Printed and bound in Canada by Hignell Printing Limited

Canadian Cataloguing in Publication Data

White, Paul, 1950–
Owen Sound: the port city

Includes bibliographical references.
ISBN 1-896219-23-3

1. Owen Sound (Ont,)–History. I. Title

FC3099.O94W44 2000   971.3'18   C00-932337-6
F1059.5.O94W44 2000

THE CANADA COUNCIL | LE CONSEIL DES ARTS
FOR THE ARTS | DU CANADA
SINCE 1957 | DEPUIS 1957

Natural Heritage/Natural History Inc. acknowledges the support received for its publishing program from the Canada Council Block Grant Program and the assistance of the Association for the Export of Canadian Books, Ottawa.

*This book is dedicated to
Tara, Rebecca and Bronwyn,
my wonderful daughters*

ACKNOWLEDGEMENTS

The journey to produce this book has been long and sometimes frustrating. But there have been many people along the route who have provided guidance, advice and encouragement. To those people I am truly grateful.

The idea to write a history of my home town was generated while I was writing a book about the maritime history of Georgian Bay. My best friend and co-author on the project, Larry Turner, constantly encouraged me to write this book. Unfortunately, Larry will not see the finished book as he passed away suddenly at the age of 45. However, every time I sat down to work on the book I felt his presence.

The information used in this book came from many different sources. The rich collection of Owen Sound newspapers on microfilm at the Owen Sound Library were of primary importance. I would like to thank Andrew Armitage, Janet Iles and the rest of the staff of the library for their assistance in helping me find the information and documents that I needed.

Andrew Armitage not only provided me with valuable assistance and encouragement while I was at the library, but the books that he wrote concerning various incidents in Owen Sound's history were of immense value.

The books by Melba Croft, a noted Owen Sound historian, were of great assistance in the process of preparing the manuscript. Many

ACKNOWLEDGEMENTS

times when I was unable to find a date or name from Owen Sound's past I was able to confidently turn to one of her books and find the needed information. Mrs. Croft's tenacity and thoroughness as a researcher are unparalleled. The world of historical research needs more people like Melba Croft.

There is very little information about the first decade of Owen Sound's existence (1840–50). Therefore, I was extremely pleased to find a copy of the memoirs of A.M. Stephens to describe this time period in greater detail. Stephens is also an important figure in the early years of Owen Sound's history. He helped blaze the trail for the Garafraxa Road, he worked in the community when it was only a small clearing in the wilderness and he served terms as mayor of the town and many years as a councilor.

Some aspects of Owen Sound's history do not appear to be as well documented as others. I wish to thank Paula Niall who allowed me to interview her and provided me with valuable material about the African American community of Owen Sound. I hope that one day Paula will write the definitive story of this group of people. As well, I thank Lorraine Brown; Katharine Hooke of Peterborough; Susan McNicol, Curator of the Perth Museum; Peter Meyler of Orangeville and Telfer Wegg of Neustadt for willingly sharing their resources.

The work of many other historians were also of much benefit to me in the writing of this book. Their names and their books are identified in the endnotes.

On a more personal level there are many people that I would like to thank for their encouragement and assistance.

Barry Penhale and Jane Gibson of Natural Heritage Books were constantly a source of encouragement. Their dedication to the concept of publishing quality local history books is exceptional.

My good friend Jim Algie who is an outstanding writer and a knowledgeable student of the history of this area performed not one, but two edits of the manuscript and his ideas and encouragement were much appreciated.

I would like to thank my assistant at the Grey County Archives, Jerri-Lynn Mills, who made many great suggestions about making the book more "technologically friendly" for the publisher, as well as helping me with some of the final preparations.

Wayne Landen and Joan Hyslop of the Grey County Museum were

ACKNOWLEDGEMENTS

a rich source of information and provided many of the photographs that can be found within the pages of this book.

During the past five years I have written a local history column in the Owen Sound *Sun Times* and I would like to take this opportunity to thank the many readers of that column for their telephone calls and letters many of which have led to new columns as well as ideas for this book.

I would also like to thank two very special people who have always encouraged me to write and follow my dream. They are my aunt, Marie Henderson, of Owen Sound and my uncle, Ken Rowe, who even though he lives in Edmonton, Alberta, has maintained a keen interest in the history of the area and has constantly encouraged me in this project.

My parents, Bill and Freida White, were not only a source of encouragement, but also a wealth of information about the history of Owen Sound.

My wonderful daughters, Tara, Becki and Bronwyn, for whom this book is dedicated have been a constant inspiration.

Last, and certainly not least, I would like to thank the person who has been a consistent source of encouragement and support in this project, my wife Judy. She is truly my best friend in life. As well as the encouragement that she provided she also read the manuscript an amazing twelve times! Her quiet determination and enthusiasm helped me over some of the rough spots that every author encounters.

To all those who helped in so many ways I am grateful, but, in the final analysis, the responsibility for accuracy is mine.

Contents

CONTENTS

OWEN SOUND

PROLOGUE

Three men pushed through dense underbrush, hardly noticing the blaze of autumn reds, yellows and oranges in the canopy overhead. It was early October, 1840. John Telfer and two companions had arrived in southern Georgian Bay to search out government surveyor Charles Rankin. At a Native settlement on the northwest shore of Owen's Sound, they learned that a white man had pitched camp a short distance to the south and east of the river which entered the bay at its apex.

The trio's energy and enthusiasm were flagging by the time they spotted smoke from the Native encampment. They had journeyed a long way, riding wagons at first on rough settlement roads, walking later across portages to Georgian Bay's shore. From there, they had sailed and paddled into the bay Natives called Keche Weequo Doong (the Great Bay).[1]

Their shoulders and spirits sagged when Natives at this camp told them there was no white man in the village. However, just as quickly as they had slumped, their spirits soared, when in the next breath they learned of a white man camped nearby.

They set out immediately, crossing a stream the Indians called the "noisy" river, on through the tangled maze of underbrush and fallen trees. As they continued, their bodies aching, they anticipated the end of their exhausting journey. This thought, perhaps, or the cool bite of autumn air eased their tired limbs.

John Telfer arrived in the Owen Sound area in 1840. He first served as land agent, working with surveyor Charles Rankin to establish lots for the original settlers. *Courtesy Grey County Archives.*

Suddenly they came upon a wigwam in a small clearing. There was no one around! Nothing but a horn sitting on a recently-cut stump. Legend goes that Telfer went forward, picked up the instrument, and blew.

Shortly, Charles Rankin emerged from the wilderness forest. He had been at work, marking out plots for a proposed settlement. In 1836, Rankin had been commissioned by the colonial government, not only to map out this new community, but also to survey a route from Guelph to the Georgian Bay frontier. However, the Upper Canadian Rebellion in 1837 had delayed Rankin's mission.

Finally, in the summer of 1840 Rankin began his survey in the vicinity of the Native community on the west shore of the bay. However, when the local Aboriginal population expressed displeasure at his presence, he discreetly took his surveying chains to the east bank of the Sydenham River.[2] It was here that the newcomers found him on October 7, 1840.

Like Rankin, Telfer held a government commission to open up this region. It would be his duty to act as land agent for the new settlement. He would oversee the building of roads and distribution of the lots surveyed by Rankin. Telfer also would supervise the construction of a school/church and houses in the nearby Native village.

Like the cavalry bugler's call to charge, Telfer's blowing of the horn in the small clearing signified the launching not only of a new community, but of a quest to create a port which would, for a time, dominate maritime commerce on Georgian Bay. This October 7, 1840 meeting in a wilderness clearing initiated the forces which, in working together would forge the modern community of Owen Sound!

ABORIGINALS OF THE AREA

harles Rankin and John Telfer's historic meeting signified the beginning of European settlement in this region. They, however, were not the first people to live here! The Natives whom Rankin, and then Telfer, met on the western shore of the bay were part of a civilization which had called this region home for many centuries.[1]

Prior to the opening of European settlement, several Aboriginal nations had lived here. The arrival of French explorers in the early 1600s signalled the beginning of fur trading and the Natives, especially the Hurons, formed commercial alliances with the French. The quest for furs brought the Hurons, and others allied with the French, into conflict with Iroquois traders who had commercial ties with British merchants established to the south of the Great Lakes.

In 1649, the Iroquois almost totally annihilated the Hurons of this region in a fierce trade war. Perhaps fearing a similar fate, the Huron's allies migrated to the north and west. For the next half century, the Iroquois used the Owen Sound/Bruce Peninsula region, then known as Indian Peninsula, as their own hunting grounds.

Around 1700, however, the Ojibwa and other former allies of the devastated Huron nation returned and routed the Iroquois in a bloody series of battles. With the Iroquois out of the area, the Wahbadick, Newash, Wahwahnosh, and Metegwob tribes of the Ojibwa nation [2] returned to their former land and lived in relative tranquility for the rest of the 1700s.[3]

However, the first decades of the 19th century marked the impending end of Aboriginal dominion. The colonial government of Upper Canada realized it needed more land to meet increasing demands from settlers arriving in North America. One strategy for acquisition was to draft a series of treaties and present them to the Natives in order to "legally" lay claim to Native lands for settlement.

The man leading this campaign was Sir Francis Bond Head, the governor of Upper Canada. Using the guise of concern for the Natives, Bond Head plotted to remove the Aboriginals from contact with white settlers. Writing in 1836, Bond Head stated "the Indian breathes pure air, beholds splendid scenery, traverses unsullied water, and subsists on food which, generally speaking, forms not sustenance but the manly amusement, as well as occupation, of his life." [4] He also voiced concern about the impact of foreign diseases and alcohol on the Native population.

This rationale led Bond Head to conclude that Indians could never be civilized. Consequently, the governor determined that isolation from white society was in their best interest. At first he proposed small isolated reservations, but in the end he aspired to relegate all Natives to exile on Manitoulin Island.[5]

Although Bond Head's ultimate goal was to remove all First Nations people to Manitoulin, he first had to wrest control of the land from them in order to facilitate settlement of the Owen Sound region. In 1836, a treaty was negotiated which helped create a tract of land to begin the proposed non-native settlement. It also designated tracts of land as Native territory "in perpetuity." "However, in the next quarter of a century, 'forever' proved to be something other than the standard dictionary meaning." [6]

The 1836 treaty reduced Native land territory from over two million acres to approximately 450,000 acres.[7] However, as the community of Owen Sound and other area settlements grew, the colonial government exerted further pressure on the Aboriginals to give up even more territory. As a result, in the 1840s and 1850s more "treaties" were signed and the indigenous populations were forced onto smaller and more remote tracts of land.

By 1842, as the number of settlers increased in the area, Native leaders began to feel encroachment on the lands which they had long considered their domain. A tenuous, contentious situation was developing with the Aboriginals clinging to their traditional lifestyle in the face of increasing demands from settlement.

In response to this situation, Chief Senegal of Newash decided that his community would leave their village on the west shore of Owen's Sound. At first, they relocated on a reserve on Colpoys Bay, but it was not long before they moved again, this time further up the Bruce Peninsula to Cape Croker.

There is a certain irony in this decision to move away from the influence of the white settlers. The Chief's daughter, Nah-nee-bah-wee-quay, (translated meaning: Upright Woman) who was nine years old at the time, convinced her father to allow her to stay and further her education! Later, when she married an English minister and teacher, William Sutton, the Natives of the area presented them with a parcel of land immediately south of Presque Isle, a small coastal port 15 km north of Owen Sound on the west shore of the bay. Despite the fact the couple built a home and farm buildings on this land,

Nah-nee-bah-wee-quay, daughter of Chief Senegal of Newash, married William Sutton. Also known as Catherine Sutton, she travelled to England to meet Queen Victoria in an attempt to resolve a land dispute. *Courtesy County of Grey-Owen Sound Museum.*

ensuing treaties failed to recognize their ownership and the property was dispersed in a land auction. Although the Suttons received support from both the white and Native communities, the government continued to refuse to recognize their claim to ownership.

Nah-nee-bah-wee-quay, or Catherine Sutton (as she was also known) was a determined woman. She decided to go to England and present her case to Queen Victoria! In 1859, she toured the Canadian colony and northern United States seeking support for her claim and money to finance her trip across the Atlantic. The next year, 1860, she left for England. In June, she was given an audience with the Queen.

Catherine Sutton admitted later that she had been so nervous at the meeting she had momentarily forgotten how to bow and kiss the Queen's hand. Victoria promised that when Crown Prince Albert travelled to Canada he would investigate the situation. However, nothing resulted from the Prince's visit. The frustrated Suttons, however, were able to buy back some of their land. But unfortunately, Nah-nee-bah-wee-quay would enjoy only a short time on her property. She died in 1865, just five years after her presentation to Queen Victoria. The grave of Nah-nee-bah-wee-quay (Catherine Senegal Sutton) can be found just a few metres south of the Presqu'ile Road off Grey County Road #1. It overlooks Georgian Bay at Sutton Point, only twelve kilometres north of the Owen Sound business section.

To understand why the Sutton's lost their land, it is important to know what was going on in the 1850s in terms of the Native ownership of land in the area. During this period the ownership of property north of present-day Highway #21, between Owen Sound and Southampton, was in question. Increased pioneer settlement had threatened the insularity of Native communities. Already the considerable growth of Owen Sound had been the catalyst for the Newash settlement to relocate at Cape Croker.

Decisions had to be made. Who owned this land? The Indian Peninsula, now known as the Bruce Peninsula, had been designated Native territory through a previous treaty. In 1857, in order to further the growth of settlement in Owen Sound, the lands which had been the village of Newash were taken over, and the settlement north of the Pottawatomi River was named Brooke or Brookholm.

These actions established and defined the geographical framework from which the community of Owen Sound would grow and prosper.

2

A CLEARING IN THE WILDERNESS

n the years following Rankin and Telfer's historic meeting, settlers
by the hundreds came to the mouth of the Sydenham River on
Owen's Sound. Like so many pioneers who had come to the New
World they had dreams for a new future. The prospect of owning
their own land, and making a better life for themselves and their families, had driven them to seek a place where they could carve a home
from the wilderness, initially for survival, and later, it was hoped, prosperity.

Some came with little more than a few possessions and the clothes
that they wore. Others came with some merchandise or equipment to
start businesses. All came with a dream that ultimately would form
their new community.

The pioneer's first priority was to build a shelter and to clear the
land. Their first homes were roughly assembled using the easiest available materials, sod and timber. Historian E.C. Guillet described the
living conditions in one of these early pioneer shanties through a quote
from a Mrs. Cook in Bruce County, "the shanty to which we went had
a bark roof, and this roof leaked so badly that when it rained my hus-
band had to hold an umbrella over us when we were in bed."[1]

Lots had to be cleared, not only to make room for a house and to
grow crops for sustenance, but to meet the requirements imposed by
the colonial government's land grant system. As more land was
cleared, more durable houses were erected and a few commercial

A depiction of early settlement illustrating the rough-hewn log house and shed, the number of stumps in the partially cleared patch of land, and the denseness of the surrounding forest. *From* The Pioneer Farmer and Backwoodsman. Vol. 2. *by E.C. Guillet.*

Heavy work was part of daily life of pioneer women. The making of potash in a large iron kettle was typical pioneer industry. *Illustration by C.W. Jeffries.*

establishments were built from timber that the forest provided. Gradually a community developed. With this sense of community came a desire to grow and prosper.

Life was not easy for these early settlers in Owen Sound. They had left homes in the British Isles and elsewhere to escape famine, loss of land or other hardships. Many did not possess the skills or tools needed to clear the land and build their homes. Out of this common situation, however, grew a sense of care and concern among new neighbours. They shared lodgings, labour and, when necessary, food.

They helped one another construct dwellings and shelters for livestock. Together they cleared the land. Those who possessed certain skills, shared their knowledge and helped others. In times of poor or uncertain crops, families gave willingly to others in need. Early journals and diaries relate tales of soup bones being passed from one kettle to the next, until there was little or no nourishment left in the parched bone. Such mutual dependence fostered the sense of community.

Geographically the settlement at Owen Sound was essentially isolated from the rest of Upper Canada. Prior to 1840, there are few indications of European visits to the region. The French explorer, Samuel de Champlain is said to have visited the area in 1619. As well, there is speculation by some historians that Jesuit missionaries spent time with Natives who lived at the mouth of the Saugeen River in the early 1600s. The French clerics may have also travelled to the Native community located north and west of the original Owen Sound townsite.[2]

There is also speculation that a community of French settlers existed on the east shore of the bay between Owen Sound and Leith,[3] before Rankin and Telfer arrived in 1840. However, this notion relies mainly on early settler reports of families with French names who seem to have sustained themselves by means of fishing and trapping.

The first British visitors, other than sailors on war ships during conflict with the Americans between 1812 and 1814, were most likely those who accompanied Captain William Fitz William Owen as part of the Bayfield survey team which charted this section of Georgian Bay in 1815. It is suspected by some historians that in the spring of 1824, Sir John Franklin, Lieutenant George Back, Dr. Richmond and other members of the expedition, passed through the area when they left Pene-tanguishene on their way to find the North West

William Fitz William Owen was the British Navy Officer assigned to survey Georgian Bay. He named the sound on which the city Owen Sound sits after himself. *Courtesy County of Grey-Owen Sound Museum.*

Passage in the Canadian Arctic.[4] Ironically, one of the men who would be chosen later to try and find the ill-fated Franklin expedition, William Kennedy, in 1849 owned a fishery at the mouth of the Saugeen River just twenty miles from Owen Sound.[5] In 1851, Sir John Ross, returning from the Arctic, spent an overnight stay in Owen Sound on his way back to England to report yet another failed attempt to find Franklin and his crew.[6]

Limited early exploration reflected the difficulty of travel to the area. Access by water was restricted by the long winter freeze-up of

Georgian Bay. Dense forest limited overland passage; not only was there heavy forest cover, but many of the trees were of gigantic proportions.

An example of the immensity of some of the trees that met the blade of the settler's axe, was recorded during the winter of 1847–1848. A soft elm measuring eight feet in diameter at the ground, seven feet in diameter at the stump, and ninety feet in height was felled near Annan, a few miles northeast of Owen Sound. Four expert axemen toiled for an entire morning to bring this behemoth to the ground.[7] A settler might find as many as three or four gigantic trees, to the acre. Other trees of smaller, varying sizes normally clustered around their larger cousins.

The settlers soon learned small tricks which enabled them to improve in axemanship. For instance, the axe was ground sharper in summer and left with a blunter edge in winter. This technique was necessary because the wood froze in winter. When an excessively sharpened edge became chilled, it broke easily upon contact with its frozen target.[8]

Even once settlement began, land travel remained a problem, due in part to the difficulty of building good roads. Out of necessity many early arrivals walked into the region. Ox-drawn wagons in summer and sleds in winter provided the only other means of bringing supplies and people in or out.

Such isolation furthered a sense of kinship among inhabitants, but, as well, it limited communication with those in other areas of the Owen Sound region.

3

JOHN TELFER, LAND AGENT

Working with the surveyor Rankin, Telfer, the land agent laid out plots for settlement and also oversaw the construction of a building which would serve as his residence and headquarters. This structure, which was located near the present site of Owen Sound's City Hall, was essentially two buildings connected by a covered passageway. Here supplies were stored and incoming settlers found accommodation until they could provide their own abode. Some of the community's first religious services and school classes would also be held in this building.

In mid-November 1840, John Telfer left the Sydenham valley for the winter. The next spring, he returned with his sixteen-year-old daughter, Elizabeth, to take up residence in the new settlement. Thomas Rutherford,[1] who had journeyed to the area with Telfer, however, remained over that first winter to set up and maintain a government store and warehouse to serve the needs of the settlers who were expected to arrive and begin establishing homes. Consequently, Rutherford became the first permanent European citizen of this community.

Pioneer settlements were essentially cashless societies, dependent upon barter or credit secured to future harvests. Therefore, Rutherford, who was responsible for the goods issued to him by the government, had to keep track of distribution to enable the collection of debts.

One story has passed down through the generations of an incident involving Rutherford's attempt to exact payment for supplies from some area Natives. After the passage of time this story seems quite humorous. However, at the time the situation appeared, no doubt, anything but comedic.

One day a number of Aboriginal people had arrived at the government store. Because of a language difficulty, neither they, nor the storekeeper really understood each other. The Native shoppers gathered up their goods and prepared to leave, seemingly without paying. To stop the supposed "shoplifters," the diminutive Rutherford delivered a blow to the jaw of the individual who seemed to be leader of the group. As the man collapsed, Rutherford grabbed him by the neck and dragged him out the door. The man regained his composure and attempted to run away, but tripped on a log and fell. He remained motionless on the ground, convincing both his compatriots and Rutherford that he was dead. Using signs, the other Natives communicated that their friend should be buried where he lay. Rutherford ran for a shovel and started to throw dirt on the prone Indian. The man jumped up and, with a shout, ran to the river and swam to freedom![2]

By 1841, the new settlement was taking shape in an ever-expanding clearing. Although the Native village of Newash was not far away, the two communities were separated by dense bush and the formidable barrier of the Sydenham River. The only easily accessible crossing was to the south of the new community, at the present-day site of the mill dam on 2nd. Avenue West. Here, a tree had been felled and travellers could pass over the river by walking on the bridge created by the fallen log. From the river's west bank, a blazed trail led to the Native village. This pathway also connected with another trail leading west to another Native community located at the mouth of the Saugeen River on Lake Huron.

A fear of getting lost in the dense bush and, perhaps, uncertainty about the friendliness of their Native neighbours, made early settlers wary of straying far from their clearing. To help travellers find their way, guns were fired at regular intervals in the community enabling them to follow the sound, and thereby find their destination.

As settlers arrived and began clearing lands, the dense forests were gradually diminished. Some pioneers worked on their new plots during fair weather seasons and returned for the winter to existing homes elsewhere in the Upper Canadian colony. However, this was not always a wise practice. During these winter absences, others sometimes took up these semi-developed tracts and then refused to move when the original settlers returned in the spring. Situations such as this caused

It could take up to seven years before stumps were sufficiently decayed to permit ploughing. Most settlers could not wait that long. Many stumps were burned, others were used to create stump fences. *George W. Douglas Collection, courtesy Katharine Hooke.*

difficulties for the land agent who was often called upon to adjudicate land disputes.

By 1842, what is now Eighth Street East in Owen Sound had been cleared to the top of the hill. That same year, the colonial government built a school in the Newash community and, in the next year, 1843, classes were also conducted in the government building.

The density of the bush and the difficulty met by those trying to hew a settlement from it, was illustrated when Ezra Brown, a tanner from Montreal, made it known that he wished to build a tannery at the townsite. The community leaders, not wishing to have such a foul-smelling industry in their midst, forced an unhappy Brown to locate a good trek through the bush from the community. Ironically, the then remote location designated for the tannery was in the vicinity of the modern-day intersection of 10th Street and 2nd Avenue East. It is now the very heart of modern Owen Sound's commercial district and just two short blocks from where the founding community had first begun![3]

Part of Charles Rankin's 1836 mandate had been to mark out the Garafraxa Road, which would later become Highway #6. This route would provide overland access from the south via Guelph and Fergus to the new community at the head of Owen's Sound. Without this passageway, new settlers to the area would have to face the arduous trek without benefit of a cleared land route, unless they travelled by water. Early in 1840, the work of clearing the Garafraxa Road from its southern terminus was begun. One of the labourers on this project was a young man named A. M. (Alexander Maitland) Stephens.

Upon his first visit to what would become Owen Sound, Stephens decided that he would take up residency in the new community, and would remain here for the rest of his life. An active participant in the development of Owen Sound, he was a businessman and politician, serving terms as mayor and many years as a town councillor.

Alexander Maitland (A.M.) Stephens worked on the construction crew building the Garafraxa Colonization Road. In 1842, he became a resident of Owen Sound and would become an important figure in the municipal life of the community. *Courtesy County of Grey-Owen Sound Museum.*

In 1873, Stephens wrote his memoirs, *The Early Days in Owen Sound*, and these recollections illustrate the difficulty met by those trying to make their way to the new community. The townsite of Arthur marked the beginning of the tract of land, extending westward to Lake Huron and north to Georgian Bay, which the government wished to open up to settlement. Stephens described the territory as follows:

"…a howling wilderness…as we were nightly surrounded by bands of wolves which sometimes came so close as to appear desirous of cultivating an all too intimate acquaintance. I cannot exactly say that I was afraid, but somehow or other the sensation was something like that produced by the bagpipes—the further away, the more agreeable the music." [4]

Road clearing crew members worked under difficult circumstances. Stephens was required to carry a fifty-pound pack on his back, as well as an axe and a blanket for a two day march of fifteen miles from Arthur to the location of the present-day town of Mount Forest. From here he worked his way northward, clearing trees for a wage of fifty cents a day.

The winter season was ideal for working across the frozen swamps and rivers, as well as providing opportunities for employment for many farmers and their sons who were always in need of cash employment. Each man carried a flint, a supply of spunk wood and a knife for cutting tobacco, bread and pork. Breakfast was eaten in time to begin clearing at daybreak. Dinner and supper were the same as breakfast—bread and pork. As the cook and his helpers carried dinner to the crew at their work site, the cooked pork often arrived frozen! Following the meal, the cook and his assistants would break camp and move northward about four miles. There they would set up a new camp, build a fire, prepare supper for the arrival of the crew and cut boughs of hemlock in abundance to be used as bedding for the night's rest.

This was the daily routine until the crew made camp about seventeen miles from their ultimate destination, the new settlement at the mouth of the Sydenham River. That evening, the cook informed the group that there was not enough food for the next day. In the discussion that followed, it was decided that they would stop clearing the route and march to the fledgling settlement and get supplies from the government store. The next day, after a breakfast of crude bread, the men trudged the seventeen miles in knee-deep snow and freezing temperatures.

Nightfall found the future mayor of Owen Sound and his fellow crew members on the hill to the east of the settlement. Tired and hungry, they settled in for the night at an abandoned Indian maple sugar camp. To feed the exhausted men, the cook melted snow in a pail and, after adding hog-fat, boiled two partridges which the foreman had shot during their trek.[5]

The next day they descended the hill and found the land agent's quarters. After a day's rest, the crew set out on the return journey to Arthur, leaving the rest of the route to be cleared at a later date.

The following spring, in 1842, A.M. Stephens returned to the settlement at the head of Owen's Sound to take up permanent residence. Writing later in life, he described, with a note of irony, the community as he found it that spring:

"An opening in the bush about an acre in extent, partially cleared, three log houses, one occupied by the Crown Lands Agent [Telfer] and his family, one for the accommodation of emigrants, and the third kept as a tavern by Hugh Gunn Campbell; about half-a-mile of street now called Union Street, with the timber chopped down but not cleared off; a deep, dark, and winding river, having a dense growth of cedar on either side with tops interlacing over head; forming the only channel of communication with the outside world and looking very unlike the future home of iron steamships."[6]

THE FLY, GEORGIAN BAY SCHOONER

n 1842, Charles Rankin officially named the settlement, Sydenham, in honour of Charles Poulett Thomson, Lord Sydenham, who served as the Governor of Canada from 1839 to 1841. According to historian, Allan Ross, the land agent, John Telfer, had wanted to name the new community, Edinburgh. However, local pride and the customs of a new land were too strong and his suggestion was ignored.[1] In 1842, the newly named community welcomed many new settlers and more buildings appeared in the ever-expanding forest clearing. Among the notable new edifices were the previously mentioned tannery of Ezra Brown and the store and residence of W. C. Boyd.

Boyd was perhaps the first of the pioneer entrepreneurs who realized that the growth and well-being of the community was interlinked with his own commercial aspirations. In order to transport his family and supplies from Toronto to their new home, Boyd had purchased the fifteen ton schooner, the *Fly*.[2] In 1842, there was no direct, economical land transport to bring supplies and settlers into the pioneer community. Boyd recognized this fact and the *Fly* became the first of an armada of Great Lake vessels which would eventually call this community its home port.

Upon his arrival at Sydenham, Boyd maintained a hired crew of three to sail the *Fly*. After several trips to Coldwater and Goderich for supplies, Boyd told the crew that Stephens, who had been in his employ since the latter's arrival in the settlement, would be joining them for a voyage to Detroit. For some reason, two of the crew members, Duncan and Alexander McNabb, refused to sail and left Boyd's employ. The third, Isaiah Chokee, remained.

Isaiah Chokee was an Owen Sound pioneer in his own right. As an African he may indeed have been the first black citizen of this community. He had been kidnapped in Africa, but instead of being sold into slavery in the Americas, he had been kept on board a man-of-war for fourteen years. While his ship was in the port of New York, Chokee had slipped ashore and made his way to Toronto where he was hired by Boyd to serve as cook and general labourer on the *Fly*.[3]

In the early 1840s, the few settlers in the area spent their days desparately trying to survive in an environment hostile to their encroachment. Most of their time involved clearing land and building accommodations for their families and the few animals which each possessed. Growing crops in those initial years was difficult at best, as stumps and fallen trees from the clearing process impeded abundant crop production. This subsistence-level farming, however, was not yet enough to sustain the local establishment of commercial milling of wheat into flour. Therefore, flour, like many other necessities of life, often had to be transported into the community.

There were two means of acquiring large amounts of flour. One was to travel to St. Vincent, a settlement about fifteen miles to the east of Owen Sound in the general proximity of the modern-day town of Meaford, and purchase wheat for about one dollar a bushel[4] then take it to Coldwater for grinding. The other method was to sail to Coldwater and then travel overland to Newmarket, just north of Toronto, purchase flour, and transport it back to Coldwater and on to the *Fly*, a journey which took about a week to complete.

Wheat grown in the Owen Sound area was not always shipped by schooner to be ground into flour. Some settlers transported their grain overland to Belfountain in the Georgetown area after a grist mill was erected at that community. Although this route was shorter in distance, it was probably not as convenient for some as sending it to Coldwater. To transport the grain overland, oxen were hooked up to a wooden sleigh known as a "jumper."

Others relied upon coffee mills to hand grind their wheat into flour, a most tedious and laborious task. Some early journals report that a whole day of grinding by hand with a coffee mill would produce a little more than enough flour for a loaf of bread. E.C. Guillet reported that one early settler to Grey County stated that men would rather "...chop all day in the bush than grind a half a bushel of wheat in the old coffee mill."[5] Consequently, this labour was often delegated to the women and children of the family.

Ultimately, to fulfill the growing need for a mill in the area, one was erected in the early 1840s at Inglis Falls, a few miles to the south of the community of Sydenham. In 1846, another mill was contracted to be built a few miles to the north, on the east shore of the bay at Leith.[6]

In 1842, a year when flour was particularly scarce in the settlement, Boyd seconded Stephens to sail with him and Chokee to Coldwater to replenish the rare commodity. This marked the beginning of Stephens's somewhat reluctant sailing career aboard the *Fly,* and his recollections of sailing provide us with some insight into the perils of the early period of shipping on Georgian Bay. These intrepid sailors on Georgian Bay waters faced many dangers, as he would learn on his second trip, this time with Archibald MacNab and Isaiah Chokee as crew mates.

They had sailed to St. Vincent, purchased wheat and were headed for Coldwater to have it milled. As the vessel approached the gap near Christian Island, the winds on the bay freshened. At sundown, the sky began to darken and bolts of lightning flared on the horizon. After MacNab and Chokee retired below deck, Stephens became concerned about the severity of the approaching storm. He called to MacNab who stuck his head and shoulders above deck, looked about and remarked that "...he thought there would be more noise than wool, as the devil said when he shaved the pig."[7]

He had no sooner made this remark and returned below deck to his bed, when the gale struck with such a force that the *Fly*, with all its canvas up, was thrown on her end beams. Fortunately, in the same instant the ship righted herself. Stephens recalled thinking that:

"With the night as dark as pitch, the rain coming down in torrents, the sea making a clean sweep over us, the wind howling, the thunder roaring and lightning flashing, I can scarcely be laughed at for wishing myself safe on shore." [8]

MacNab came on deck and took the helm while Chokee came up to help Stephens shorten the sail. Stephens' narrative continues:

"Isaiah loosened the flying-jib sheet, but got into such a flurry that

21

he let it slip out of his hands and in trying to catch it again the block struck him on the head, knocking him flat on the deck. If my head had received the blow I think the storm would have troubled me no longer, but his, being about as hard as the block, did not appear to be affected thereby, for he quickly gathered himself up and succeeded in securing the sheet and stowing the jib. We finally managed to get all the other sails under close reef."[9]

Due to the darkness of the night, they could no longer see to navigate through the gap, so elected to remain where they were for the night. The next morning, in the storm's tranquil aftermath, the damage was assessed. One of the jaws of the main gaff had been wrenched from its moorings and lay on the deck with its long spikes exposed. Likewise, the foremast had snapped but remained in place, held only by the stays and shrouds. Stephens recalled thinking that:

"Considering the violence of the storm and the fact of its striking us with all sail set, the wonder is that either the deck was not swept clean, or the ship sent to the bottom with sails, spars and rigging, hands, cargo and cook."[10]

In spite of this near disaster and the considerable damage, the men continued on to Coldwater. The urgency of returning home with a load of flour and supplies outweighed the difficulty of sailing a crippled vessel!

Upon their return to Sydenham, the flour was sold for six dollars a barrel. The fact that few in the community had cash in great amounts did not stop Boyd from passing out supplies to all who had a need, payment could equally be through either barter or credit. Stephens stated that he "...never knew Boyd to refuse provisions to a family in want, but on the contrary I [Stephens] have known him to be often imposed upon by those who had money but concealed it, and obtained credit by working upon his sympathies."[11] This trip to Coldwater had been particularly fraught with disaster, not only had the vessel had been severely damaged, but the crew had almost lost their lives. As well, due to a lack of cash-paying customers, Boyd had most likely not shown a profit on the venture. Yet, when the community was once again in need of flour, Boyd turned to Stephens and asked him to sail to Coldwater for supplies. When Stephens objected to the unprofitability of such a trip, Boyd admonished him saying that "...the settlers must have flour and if he did not furnish it they would starve."[12]

Reluctantly, Stephens relented and set out for Coldwater. By nightfall he had reached the furthest point on the northeast shore of Owen's Sound. It had started to rain and, with winds coming hard from the east, there was little chance of the *Fly* making much headway during the night. Not surprisingly, the crew, did not wish to spend the night on deck in such conditions. Stephens recalled that "...we stowed all the canvas except the foresail, which we close-reefed and close-hauled, and lashed the helm hard-up, or hard-down, (I forget which)"[13] and retired below deck for the night. Upon awaking in the morning they found that they had drifted a long way off their intended course; they were north of Cape Croker! Fortunately, they had somehow missed being wrecked on Griffith Island! The men returned to their route and continued their mission without further incident.

The onset of winter in 1842 once more isolated the new community from the rest of the world. However, "...thanks to Boyd and the schooner *Fly*, it was well supplied with provisions, and if the dwellings were not frost-proof, firewood was plentiful, so that there was no danger of either starving or freezing."[14]

A formal portrait of W.C. Boyd. His schooner, the *Fly* braved the treacherous waters of Georgian Bay to provide early Owen Sound settlers with a transportation link with the rest of the colony. *Courtesy County of Grey-Owen Sound Museum.*

W.C. Boyd's influence seems to have gone beyond the white settlement. Natives at the nearby village made him an honourary member of the tribe and bestowed upon him a name which meant the Beaver. His daughter was called Wanhingoon, or Wild Rose.[15]

During the winter of 1842–43, Stephens was required to travel to Toronto to carry out business for his employer, Boyd. With Georgian Bay covered with ice, his only means of transportation was by foot, which meant his walking for several days. On his return trip, he visited friends and family who expressed their dismay, or perhaps, disapproval of his chosen new home. Stephens' recollections of their comments provide us with insight into the attitude that other Upper Canadians had towards the prospect, or perhaps, the folly, of settling on the Georgian Bay frontier. They seemed to have thought that Stephens was "...fond of adventure and to be one and all of the opinion that I [Stephens] would have displayed more wisdom if I had stayed on my father's farm."[16]

He reasoned that their opinions were based upon the fact that, according to a map of Upper Canada, the Sydenham settlement was "...fully a degree north..." of them and therefore colder and snowier. They surmised that the growth of "...turnips, potatoes, oats and corn, spring wheat..." might be possible on a limited basis given favourable conditions, however, to consider the possibility of producing "...fall wheat, or such fruits as apples or pears..." would be foolhardy. Furthermore, they noted that the region had "...neither roads, schools, nor churches, and [was] unlikely ever to contain a population capable of sustaining these elements of civilization..."[17] However, these opinions did not sway Stephens from his plans.

That same winter, Sydenham held its first "official" town meeting. As it was traditional that each Upper Canadian community hold a town meeting in January, the land agent had issued a summons requesting that all settlers attend Sydenham's first such meeting on the first Monday in January 1843. At this meeting Stephens entered public office, being elected to the position of town clerk.

Although no records of this formal meeting survive, Stephens recalled that the gathering resolved to bind the community to "...observe and keep all the laws and ordinances there and then enacted" and that pound keepers were elected and the settlement was divided into sections, and road masters were chosen. However, it seems that the settlers did not regard the meeting as an important event when one considers that Stephens' recalled that "...with the exception of affording us a day's amusement the meeting produced no results, the whole affair being soon forgotten." [18]

THE IMPACT OF ISOLATION

Residents in hinterland regions and those of their metropolitan centres holding economic and political power have traditionally regarded each other with disdain. Although the region depends upon the metropolis and vice versa, each seems unconscious of such mutual self-interest. It seems that during the 1840s this phenomenon attached itself to the relationship between Sydenham and Toronto.

Perhaps the distance and lack of good connecting routes between the two communities led to acrimony. It must have seemed to the pioneers on the frontier that the words and actions of those in the more settled region of the colony, showed little or no respect or sympathy for the trials of a community working to survive on the edge of the Upper Canadian wilderness.

Due to the remoteness of the area, many citizens of Sydenham and the surrounding vicinity seldom saw a newspaper and had difficulty keeping up on the news of the world. There was no direct mail service to Sydenham, the delivery terminus being Barrie. The postmaster at St. Vincent, William Stevenson, walked to Barrie, a distance of more than 50 miles, and picked up correspondence for his region. Likewise, a settler from Sydenham expecting mail had to walk to St. Vincent to pick up his letters or parcels.[1]

However, these settlers were not ignorant unlettered people. Pioneer journals and diaries relate the relish with which books were read and

Early clearings were separated by dense stands of trees, heightening the sense of isolation.
Illustration by Anne Langton, from Gentlewoman of Upper Canada.

passed among neighbours. Possibly because of the isolation settlers felt, many early diaries and reports indicated that there seems to have been a sense of caring little about the outside world with the exception of letters from the homeland. Instead, there seemed to be a feeling of pity for those who didn't know the joy of living in this region!

During the winter of 1842–43, public distaste for the political leadership of the Upper Canadian colony reached an almost frenzied state in the locality around Sydenham. Disdain peaked when it was learned that the land agents at both Arthur and Sydenham had received instructions concerning payment for granted land. The agents were to demand that each settler pay in full what was owing on his land. Failure to do so meant that the agent was to sell or grant the land, no matter how well-developed, to another potential settler. This stipulation affirmed to settlers that those in power had little regard for their plight; this was yet another contravention of the land grant agreement. They had tried to maintain their end of the bargain, however, the government had failed to meet many of its obligations.

When the region had first opened for settlement in 1840, the government told prospective settlers that a road, a full chain in width, with all rivers and streams bridged and swamps made passable, would be opened from the northeast corner of Garafraxa township to the head of Owen's Sound. Each settler was to be granted fifty acres of land and, after clearing that parcel, was eligible to purchase an adjoining fifty acres, which the government had promised to hold in reserve, at eight shillings per acre. The total cost for the reserve allotment was about eighty dollars.[2]

By 1841, the Garafraxa Road had been upgraded for fifteen miles from the south end at Arthur, and twelve miles south from Sydenham. However, because of a lack of money or, perhaps, government interest, the middle thirty-three miles remained unimproved. Most major rivers had been bridged, but creeks and swamps remained treacherous.

Indignant at the government's actions, these settlers began planning action to protect their land reserves. While they had been somewhat sympathetic to the government's lack of revenue for the completion of the Garafraxa Road, this sympathy, however, wore out with the government's planned takeover and resale of what they perceived to be their land.

At a meeting called to consider their options, the settlers elected Nathaniel Herriman to present their case to the Upper Canadian government. Perhaps as a result of this action, the land agents were ordered not to enforce the recent orders. However, these orders were not rescinded, leaving the community in a state of anxiety. Some citizens, fearing the loss of their land without some form of compensation, sold their property, often for less than its real value, to the first new settlers to arrive that spring and summer.[3]

This was not the first time there had been a contentious issue between this frontier community and representatives of the colony's more developed region. During the previous summer of 1842, the Reverend William Ryerson had paid a visit to Sydenham. At the village of Newash, he had delivered a sermon on the evils of trading liquor with the Natives. While visiting the settlement, Ryerson had been guest of honour at a banquet in the home of W.C. Boyd, one of Owen Sound's eminent citizens.

However, once Ryerson returned to Toronto, he published a report of his visit in a local newspaper. He went to great lengths to detail the hardships that he incurred in travelling to this outpost of civilization. He then went on to describe his hosts who had graciously feted him as a visiting dignitary in less than glowing terms. He illustrated "...the miserable condition in which he found the people. He spoke of [Sydenham] as being 'a small white settlement the inhabitants of which were in a state of starvation for want of temporal and spiritual food.' "[4]

Stephens recalled in his memoirs that the minister's comments had injured the pride of the settlers:

> "How he could make such statements without drawing largely upon his imagination is to me a mystery. Of a lack of temporal food he certainly saw no indication, as the table at which he was entertained he would find supplied in no grudging manner, and I feel confident that none of the inhabitants complained to him of scarcity, for nothing of the kind existed. As for spiritual food, we felt disposed to enjoy what we had and patiently wait till the improvement in our circumstances would allow us a more liberal supply."[5]

These circumstances, perhaps, created the sense in the community of wariness towards towards the centres of political and economic power in what would become the province of Ontario.

6

DETERMINATION AND INNOVATION

The entire decade of the 1840s was a period of innovation, coupled with trial and tribulation in the new settlement. Although some people may have had visions of greatness for their community, those dreams had to be put on hold while individual needs were satisfied. Survival was difficult. The long winters of isolation, made more so by inadequate land routes and frozen waterways, created a need for a combination of self-reliance and reciprocal dependence upon neighbours.

The cold winters prodded some settlers to consider a more substantial building material than the usual timber for their homes. Although there were sufficient trees to provide logs or sawn timber for house building, materials necessary to make bricks were equally in ample supply. While records do not tell of an experienced brick mason living in Sydenham in the early 1840s, however, because of pioneer ingenuity and co-operation, there was soon a good supply of bricks for construction purposes. No doubt there was much trial and error, but will and necessity prevailed.

This need for a more substantial building material would establish brick-making as an important industry in Owen Sound. By the 1850s, the community had expanded beyond its beginnings as a rugged outpost of civilization. To meet the needs of an expanding population, the Armstrong brothers established commercial kilns on the east hill south of present-day 6th Street East.

The lime kilns shown within the circle in the centre of the map were located at the current site of the Grey County Administration Building. *Courtesy County of Grey-Owen Sound Musem.*

Later, in the 1870s, the Armstrongs sold their business to James White and his sons, William and Wellington. In 1905, during an era of ambitious expansion in the area, partnerships mushroomed as businessmen moved to undertake entrepreneurial projects. James Leslie, John Legate and John Ross bought the business and created the Owen Sound Brick Company. On the west side of the Sydenham River, Robert Wyllie and William Malcolm operated the Lethbridge Brick Company. Originally a Brooke-based operation, they moved south to 4th Street, west of 6th Avenue in 1902. These owners later merged with the Owen Sound Brick Company. In the 1950s, a century after the Armstrongs had opened the first commercial brick-making enterprise, this industry would disappear from Owen Sound's commercial and industrial community.[1]

The pioneer brick makers of the 1840s needed lime to hold the bricks in place. To answer this need, a primitive lime kiln was constructed in the side of a ravine to the east of 9th Avenue East (formerly the Garafraxa Road) near the present day site of the Grey County Building and the Grey County Museum. A circular excavation was created about eight feet deep and six feet in diameter. At the bottom, an entrance was carved out of the side of the ravine. There was little danger of cave-ins because the soil was a good stiff clay. The hole was then filled with broken limestone taken from the escarpment and piled above in layers, in a conical shape. A roaring fire at the bottom of the cavity was kept burning until the stone was thoroughly burnt and all of the lime collected.[2]

While the first lime kiln operation was developed and run by pioneers in 1842–43, it was taken over by Robert Holmes and his brother, William, when they moved to the community from Guelph in 1846. A map of the area from the 1870s places four lime kilns in the immediate vicinity of the Holmes operation. All of them were located east of the Garafraxa Road and within, on average, three chains (about 61 metres) of the road. It would appear that one of these four kilns was still in operation in 1946 under the ownership of a man named Brown.

These were not the only lime kilns to operate in the area. Two others were located on the west escarpment in Owen Sound, one on 7th Street West and the other on 9th Street West, directly opposite the present day location of West Hill Secondary School. There was also a lime kiln on the farm of William Hickey, who was reputed to have been the first non-Native child born in Brooke. His birthplace was near the site of Victoria Public School on 3rd Avenue West. Hickey's farm was located on Park Street between 16th and 19th Streets in Sarawak township.[3]

An early threshing outfit. Often "gangs" of men from the immediate community became the threshers, moving from farm to farm until the harvest was complete. Feeding the threshing crew required a table laden with provisions. *From the* Pioneer Farmer and Backwoodsman Vol. 2.

In 1848, an event occurred which was sure to lighten the load of area settlers at harvest time. A crew of men with a small threshing machine came to the region. Settlers with four dollars available, could rent this labour-saving device. The machine was only six feet long and five feet wide. Its principal parts were a cylinder and a feeding board. The straw was removed from the cylinder with a rake and then thrown into the mow for use later. After two hundred sheaves had been threshed, the machine was stopped and all the grain was collected. Two hundred bushels could be threshed in a good ten hour day.[4] Considering that hand threshing would have taken much longer and been much more laborious, the settlers must have been most grateful for this new invention.

Although these technological advances certainly improved the life of the pioneers, life was still anything but comfortable.

7

The Beginning of Maritime Commerce

Sometime in 1842 or 1843, W.C. Boyd sold the *Fly*. From the beginning of Sydenham, this ship had been the settlement's main line of communication with the outside world. Although early shipping records are scarce, it is likely other vessels probably began calling at the community shortly after its inception. In his book, A.M. Stephens makes an early reference to a vessel stopping at the Newash settlement to trade. Before long, Sydenham would become a trading port. Maritime commercial traffic increased as the population of the area grew. One can also surmise that Boyd would not have sold the community's only maritime link to the rest of Upper Canada unless other boats were actively visiting this port.

These vessels arrived, either to bring new settlers or produce to the growing market, and left carrying the goods which had been produced in the developing community. In 1844, Boyd built a wharf to accommodate this increased sailing traffic. Early maps suggest that Boyd's Wharf was probably located in the area where the National Table Company was located, where the Lumley Bayshore Arena now stands.[1] This wharf marked the beginning of an era which would eventually see Sydenham, later called Owen Sound, become an important Great Lakes port.

By 1845, a sloop was sailing regularly between Sturgeon Bay, at the northern end of the Coldwater Road on the southeastern shore of Georgian Bay, to Sydenham with a stop at Penetanguishene.[2] Along with prospective settlers and produce, this vessel, and others like it also carried visitors to the area. One of these early tourists was artist Paul Kane, who arrived in 1845. He would become famous for his portraits and landscapes of frontier Canada. At Sydenham he purchased a canoe and spent time visiting and painting local Native personalities.[3]

On June 20, 1845, an important event occurred in the maritime history of the community. That day the *Gore*, the first commercial steamer to enter Owen's Sound, arrived in port. The vessel arrived from Detroit, via Goderich, amidst great fanfare. A welcoming party, including Thomas Gordon, George Brown, Messrs. Dease and Jackson, along with others sailed to Cabot's Head where they hailed the *Gore* with volleys of shotgun blasts at five o'clock in the morning.[4]

The *Gore* went into service as a vital link on the route between Toronto and Sydenham. This route involved many facets of pioneer transportation. Travellers went from Toronto to Lake Simcoe by stage coach. After sailing across Lake Simcoe, another stage carried the passengers for eighteen miles to Sturgeon Bay where they boarded the *Gore*. A seventeen mile voyage reached Penetanguishene, with the final sixty-five mile voyage taking the traveller to Owen Sound. The charge for luggage for the entire trip was six shillings per hundred-weight (6s. per cwt.).[5]

The Reverend Alphonsus William Henry Rose, whose presence in the area was previously unknown to local historians, is thought to have visited in the late 1840s. He described the *Gore* as follows:

"She has the reputation of being one of the most admirable sea-boats upon the lakes—a very necessary qualification, as Lake Huron, [Georgian Bay] from its depth and vastness, puts one more in mind of the roll of the Atlantic Ocean in a gale of wind than any of the others, except, perhaps, Lake Superior. It requires a practised eye, however, to discover the beauty of her lines, below the villainously ugly paint which they have put upon her top-hamper. She used formerly to run to the American side; and it is said that the Yankees cannot bear our genuine substantial looking black hulls, calling them 'black British sarpents.' In deference to their fancies, the upper works of the *Gore* were painted a dirty white, streaked with green and puce colour, which may have been useful, but looked anything but ornamental." [6]

Rose provides us with valuable insights into what settlers faced upon their arrival by boat at this pioneering outpost. He described rowing from the steamer for about one-half to three-quarters of a mile up the river and landing at a wharf near the Land Agent's Office. The building was "...dignified by the imposing name of the 'Government House.'"[7] He continued:

> "You are not, however, to expect to hear the crash of military music, see sentries pacing up and down, gay 'aides' dashing about, nor delicate-looking secretaries turning out for an after-noon's ride, or indeed any of the concomitants of colonial viceroyalty, as the abode in question, notwithstanding its sounding name, aspires only to the humble but truly Samaritan office of sheltering emigrants of the poorer classes till they are able to provide for themselves." [8]

Rose stated that newcomers to the area could make "...application to the authorities" in order to be housed in the building until they had made other living accommodations. The building provided the prospective settler with quarters which were "...fitted up with sleeping cribs, cooking stoves, & c., fuel being to be had for the chopping." The bulk of the goods brought by the settlers were kept locked for safekeeping in a storage area.[9]

One could take advantage of the government's hospitality free of charge "...till the house is filled, when the 'oldest inhabitant' has to turn out". Rose pointed out that "...he must be very imprudent or careless if he have not provided himself with the means of getting a roof of his own over his head before any compulsory ejectment be necessary."[10]

Sydenham added shipbuilding to its commercial enterprises when sometime between 1846 and 1848,[11] the first locally-built steamer, the *Anne McKenzie*, was built and launched. She had a one hundred foot keel with a twenty-four foot beam.[12] A local carpenter, Henry Wood, established a woodworking shop to provide those services to the shipbuilder.

The building of the *Ann McKenzie* was not without controversy. The ship's owner failed to pay one of the carpenters, perhaps Henry Wood, and this artisan hired a lawyer to trace the vessel and recoup his loses. However, in the elapsed time frame, the vessel had sailed to Toronto and left that port with a load of lumber bound for Quebec.

There were two ships by the name of the *City of Owen Sound*. This one was built at Owen Sound by John Simpson in 1874 and reportedly had the first Owen Sound-made propeller that was produced. She later sank in Lake Huron. The ship at the right is believed to be the *Waubuno*, which was last on Georgian Bay in 1879. *Courtesy County of Grey-Owen Sound Museum.*

She had then sailed across the Atlantic to Britain. Finally, the *Ann McKenzie* was located in Rio de Janeiro, far from the jurisdiction of the local sheriff![13]

Shortly after the launching of the *Ann McKenzie*, two more vessels were constructed here. The *Elizabeth Broder* plied the waters of Georgian Bay, servicing the trading needs of local port communities. The other, the *Belle McPhee*, a two-masted schooner, was originally launched about 1850. For about three years the *Belle McPhee* sailed the Great Lakes, then she was brought into Owen Sound for renovations. A third mast was erected and thirty feet were added to her length, likely by cutting her in half, with the new section being added at the mid-point. Unfortunately, a year later the *Belle McPhee* hit a rock off Thornbury and sank. Luckily the crew was saved by a fishing tug.[14]

By the end of Sydenham's first decade of existence, the community seemed to be flourishing. Settlers were clearing land and establishing homesteads, not only within the boundaries of the settlement, but also venturing into the immediate hinterlands in every direction. Reverend

Rose described how this expansion had occurred and how it had affected the cost of land.

When a surveyor laid out a new community, parcels of land called "park lots" are "…reserved in blocks of from 4 or 5 acres to 40 or 50 acres." These blocks "…encompass the town for one or two miles, or even more, and are put up to public competition at the land sales."[15]

The "park lots" must have been a land speculator's dream! Rose pointed out that at a land sale in 1846, some of these blocks sold "…at a price averaging perhaps from 12s. to 15s., or considerable upwards, an acre, but have very greatly risen in value since." A few years later, he suggested that those who then paid 20£. for their lots, would not take 100£. for them now. He wrote that "another batch are expected to come into the market in the spring of 1849."[16]

Commercial activities diversified beyond agriculturally-related industries in Owen Sound now included fishing, shipbuilding and a thriving mercantile community.

8

FROM WILDERNESS CLEARING TO
TOWN OF OWEN SOUND

n 1851, an event occurred which further illustrated that Sydenham had grown beyond a pioneering outpost. Beginning June 28, 1851, the local citizenry could now read their own community newspaper. On that date, Volume 1, Number 1 of the *Comet: Farmers' and Mechanics' Protector*, with the rather pretentious subtitle "An Agricultural, Commercial and Literary Journal" took up its role, not only as dispenser of news, but also as the promoter and booster of the development of the community. The editor was Owen Van Dusen.

Nineteenth century Ontario newspapers were unabashed promoters of their communities. With a "no holds barred" attitude, they supported local economic development and population growth. The community's prestige was paramount to the editors of these newspapers, as other communities in the area were often seen as rivals. Threats by other towns to the growth and development of the editor's town were not taken lightly. Consequently, editorial commentary was often extremely vitriolic. Thus, the establishment of a newspaper in a pioneering community was often an indicator of its economy having diversified beyond subsistence levels.

Within two years of the birth of the *Comet*, two additonal newspapers, the *Lever* owned and operated by Messrs. Campbell and Boyd representing reform political interests in the community, and the conservative *Times*,[1] whose editor was Richard Carney, had also set up their printing presses in Owen Sound. Although these publications

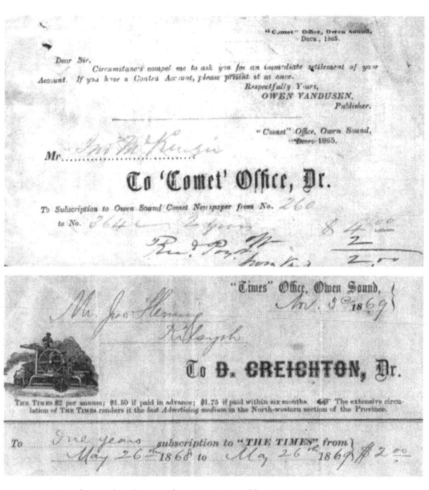

Top: An original note dated December 1865, signed by Owen Van Dusen, owner of the Owen Sound *Comet*, regarding an overdue account. *Courtesy Grey County Archives.*
Bottom: A payment from Mr. John Fleming for a year's subscription (May 1868–May 1869) to the *Times* of Owen Sound. Note the date, November 3, 1869. *Courtesy Grey County Archives.*

had differing political slants according to their views of the world, their ambitions were similar, all geared to the promotion of Owen Sound's interests in terms of economic expansion and growth.

The growth in maritime traffic to and from the community increased the visibility of settlement, and therein lay a source of confusion. Charles Rankin had named the community Sydenham almost a decade earlier, however, many referred to it by the name of the body

Being named the county seat in 1852 meant that Owen Sound was required to have a county gaol. This photo shows the gaol walls and back of the Court House. *Courtesy County of Grey-Owen Sound Museum.*

of water on which it was located, Owen Sound. In order to clarify the situation, the June 28, 1851 edition of the *Comet* reported that a prominent local merchant, John Frost, had chaired a recent meeting at which time it was decided that the community would henceforth be known as Owen Sound, rather than Sydenham.[2]

Originally, when the community had been named Sydenham in 1842, the Land Agent had proposed the name Edinburgh. This probably not only reflected loyalty to his homeland, but also the origins of many of the residents of the day. In 1851, one of the names proposed instead of Owen Sound was Dublin.[3] This name may have reflected a change in the demographic makeup of the community at that time.

By 1852, the *Comet* was trumpeting more prestige for Owen Sound. In its March 13 edition the newspaper announced the creation of Grey County, effective February 28, 1852, and the designation of this community as the county seat. The editor of the *Comet*, Van Dusen, announced this good news in the following manner:

> "We have great pleasure in publishing below the Proclamation of the Governor in Council, constituting the Owen Sound Reeves as a Provisional County Council, and appointing our good town the County Town, and the Reeves to meet here on Thursday, the 15th of April for the election of a warden." [4]

Although the area had been little more than a wilderness ten years before, the new County of Grey now boasted about 32,000 acres of cultivated land, and a population of about 13,000. The new county seat, Owen Sound, had in the same time span grown to a population of about 900 inhabitants living in an area of about 5700 acres.[5]

Four years later, on May 16, 1856, more good news was proclaimed. On that date, through an act of Parliament, the community was incorporated, effective January 1, 1857, as the Town of Owen Sound. Through hard work and foresight, the citizens of the community had transformed a small clearing in the wilderness into a busy Georgian Bay port in less than sixteen years.

9

RAILWAY INTRIGUE

Efficient and economical transportation and communication connections with the rest of the world, in general, are paramount to the growth and development of any community. This situation was particularly relevant to the settlement at Owen Sound.

The main transportation link by water on Georgian Bay had its limitations, with the Great Lakes being frozen over for many months of the year. Even during sailing season, storms made it hard to maintain schedules and threatened the loss of life and property.

The few roads which did exist were seldom passable. Heavy snow and ice made road travel laborious and treacherous in the winter. In spring, heavy rain and winter run-off, made the unbridged streams and rivers dangerous and difficult to ford. The bridges that did exist tended to be makeshift and vulnerable to washout.

Even travel to nearby communities could be almost as hazardous as to the further points located in the more southern areas of the colony. In order to forego the often dangerous sailing trip around the tip of the Bruce Peninsula, there were two options available to travellers leaving Owen Sound.

One was to sail to the location of the present-day town of Wiarton on Colpoys Bay, and portage west across the route which had been used by early French explorers and Natives to reach Lake Huron at either the mouth of the Sauble River or the Fishing Islands near the present-day community of Oliphant. This route however, would entail walking or sailing south to Southampton to await a vessel calling at that port. A more direct route would have been to trek along an Indian trail directly west from Owen Sound for about twenty miles through the forest to Southampton. The July 5, 1851 edition of the *Comet* announced the plans to build a road which, more or less, followed this latter pathway.

In 1851, a stage from Hamilton twice a week braved the treacherous conditions of the Garafraxa Road. James McLauchlan Sr. and his friend George Bell, travelled to the Owen Sound area in late 1854, following this stage route. They and thirteen other passengers left Hamilton on an 8:00 am stage on a Monday morning. After travelling for ten hours on what was called a "rock away" stage they arrived in Guelph. From this point, McLauchlan and Bell decided to walk. After passing through Elora and Fergus they headed towards Durham. At one point in their journey they met a man driving an ox-drawn cart whom they paid $1.00 to ride for five miles. After only a mile, McLauchlan decided that walking was easier than riding on the cart.

McLauchlan related that "...there were hotels about every two miles along the road." Once they arrived in Durham they "...put up in a first class" lodging place. For fifty cents they received "...a night's lodging, and supper consisting of bacon, bread and tea." To get to their sleeping quarters, they climbed a ladder to the second floor, where their beds consisted of sheepskins spread out on the floor.[1]

A week later, on the Monday following their departure from Hamilton, McLauchlan arrived in Owen Sound. He remembered that from the top of the hill by the lime kiln, located by the Garafraxa Road, one could see nothing of the community below except "...the long line of burnt hemlocks along the top of the East Hill." Once, within the town, he found a few houses, however, one thing did stand out in his memory. The mud on the main street! Although a plank ran along the street to act a sidewalk, this did not guarantee dry feet for pedestrians. McLauchlan remembered "...stepping off the plank to let a lady pass" and sinking "...so deeply into the mud that [I] pulled [my] boots off in getting out."[2]

There was also a stage which connected Toronto with Georgian Bay, at Penetanguishene, three times a week. Another connecting route was the Toronto and Sydenham Road, which today is Highway #10. However, its condition was similar to that of the Garafraxa. In order to try and improve this road in June 1852, the Provisional Council of Grey

The market square in the early 1850s, located in what would have been the centre of the town. *Courtesy County of Grey-Owen Sound Museum.*

County passed a motion to ask the government to repair and improve the Toronto and Sydenham Road.[3]

While better roads would be an improvement, a railroad connection with the more populous section of the colony was more desirable. Therefore, the April 3, 1852 edition of the *Comet* contained news which virtually leapt off its pages when it was read by Owen Sounders. The Toronto and Lake Huron Railroad had announced that it would be running a line into Barrie. The newspaper reported that the northern terminus for the line had not yet been determined. However, Owen Sound was a possible consideration.[4]

Excitement in Owen Sound about becoming the northern terminus of the new railroad was short-lived. In January 1853, it was revealed that the directors of the line had selected the "Hen and Chickens," as Collingwood harbour was then known, as the end of steel.[5] The editor of the *Comet* was outraged! Succeeding editions of that paper exhibited maps and editorials extolling the virtues of Owen Sound and castigating those who had been remiss in their failing to select Owen Sound as the northern terminus for the rail line. Grey County Council responded to news of Collingwood's selection instead of

A photograph of the market square in Owen Sound, dated July 1976, about 125 years after its beginning. *Courtesy Grey County Archives.*

Owen Sound as the northern terminus of the rail line by sending a petition to the Legislature for the building of an extension to Owen Sound of the Toronto to Guelph railroad.[6]

Throughout the 1850s a period of railroad building and expansion existed in Upper Canada, with every community wanting a line of steel to connect it with the rest of the colony. The popular belief was that the iron horse brought growth and economic expansion in the clouds of smoke and steam which billowed from its stack. Consequently, community meetings were held in many centres to examine the possibility of attracting a railroad. The *Comet* reported that Orangeville had held such a meeting and that the results were favourable to Owen Sound's quest for a railway line. They would recognize and support the benefits of a railway from Toronto to Owen Sound, travelling via Orangeville.

Amidst this frenzy to build a railroad to Owen Sound, a new controversy arose. A report from another paper reprinted in the *Comet* said that Sheriff George John Grange of Guelph had gone to Quebec to lobby for the creation of a rail line that would connect Owen Sound, Guelph and Buffalo, New York. Published accounts connected Mr. Grange with Richard Carney, a prominent local citizen, editor of the *Times* and future first mayor of Owen Sound and the Warden of Grey County in 1854 and again in 1857.

These newspaper reports raised the ire of the editor of the *Comet.*

An April 8, 1853 editorial opined that it was "...ridiculous to suppose that Mr. Carney had anything to do with Sheriff Grange" making a petition on behalf of the proposed railway. The editor went on to suggest that the involvement of American interests had not been part of Carney's strategy, but rather he considered the proposed rail line to be "...the most advantageous to Owen Sound and the country through which said line would pass..."[7]

The editorial went on to extol the virtues of a route from Toronto to Owen Sound, via Guelph, not only in terms of opening up a new route to markets for the produce from the fertile hinterland through which the line would pass, but also as the shortest direct line between Sault Ste. Marie, southern Upper Canadian towns and points in the United States.

The editorial concluded with a question concerning why the story had been published in the first place. The *Comet* wondered if indeed it had been produced "...by the selfish Toronto interests, and jealousy of Hamilton, that the line to Guelph will be too near the branch of the Great Western."[8]

When the original question was raised as to the location of the northern terminus of the Toronto and Lake Huron rail line, many meetings were held to consider Owen Sound's best strategy. It seems that Carney had petitioned community leaders not to make any financial commitments in the form of bonds or grants to entice the railway. His reasoning was that Owen Sound's harbour was superior to Collingwood's and that the railway directors would make their decision on this fact alone.

Unfortunately, this lack of action may have indeed swayed the directors of the railway company to choose Collingwood which had made a strong pitch for the railway. Almost ten years later, during a period of severe economic depression in Owen Sound, the editor of the *Comet* was lamenting the decision to follow Carney's advice and, perhaps tongue in cheek questioning Carney's motives.

In the same month it was reported that a third railway was bidding to make Owen Sound the terminus of a line from Lake Simcoe. The editor gloated that this community was about to become "the Buffalo of Canada"![9] However, the same edition also reported late-breaking news that the Guelph to Owen Sound extension had been thrown out in committee.[10]

Unfortunately for the community, a railway locomotive would not steam into town for another two decades. In the meantime, Owen Sound would develop as a centre of industry and commerce as well as supporting a growing Georgian Bay port. Growth, however, would be limited by the lack of a railway connection. During the winter months the only transportation link was a still largely unimproved network of settlement roads which were often impassable.

10

MARITIME COMMERCE

During the 1850s, maritime traffic on the Great Lakes was increasing. The Owen Sound harbour was becoming a busy place during sailing season.

In June 1851, four schooners and a steamer were moored here at the same time. Each vessel carrying cargoes of general merchandise, had taken an average of seventeen days to reach Owen Sound from Toronto. Their outgoing cargoes included a load of lumber, flour, wheat, butter, grass seed, oats and potash for Toronto.[1]

There is also some indication that the economy of the time was still not entirely driven by cash. John Frost, the entrepreneurial proprietor of a general merchandise store in the community, advertised that he not only outfitted ships with supplies, but that he also would take pelts and live cattle in lieu of cash.[2]

The combination of poor winter transportation connections and the lack of a railway, made lake shipping the focus for the survival and growth of Owen Sound. Consequently, navigation news was critical to the community. Spring months in particular, were a time of anticipation, when all eyes would turn toward the harbour and the bay, wondering when the ice would clear and the first vessel of the season would appear on the horizon.

The spring of 1852 was particularly trying for the community. Ice had lingered longer than usual. The *Comet* reported that a north wind had filled the harbour with loose ice and that a wind for a few hours from the south would soon open the harbour for ships. In the same edition, the *Comet* reported that the steamer *Belle* would arrive "...at least by the 10th of May" to begin service, connecting with the Toronto stage at southern Georgian Bay and continuing on to Sault Ste. Marie.[3]

All the news about the ships that entered port, when they arrived, departed and what cargo they were carrying would be written up in the *Comet*. One interesting article appeared in the July 2, 1852 edition of the paper:

"The schooner 'Eliza White' anchored in our harbour this morning about 6 o'clock. We observe that she has on board an unprecedented amount of freight—bringing goods to our principal merchants. Our readers may expect to see advertisements stating where goods of good quality and at low prices will hang out—from the samples that may be sent us we will judge and advise accordingly." [4]

An indication of the extent to which local farmers were producing cash crops can be seen in the May 15, 1852 edition of the *Comet* which reported that Mr. Lenfesty was shipping 3,000 bushels of wheat aboard the *Eliza White*, the beginning of the next week.[5]

One of the constant worries of a community so closely tied to maritime travel is the threat of shipwreck. The loss of life and cargo had an immediate impact on most of the community. In the 1850s, a lost ship might mean that a community would have to go without service to the outside world for a considerable length of time. The first sailing disaster to have a large impact upon Owen Sound occurred on May 16, 1852. The *Comet* reported that the steamer *Belle* had wrecked on Cape Croker.[6]

Captain McGregor, the master of the steamer, related to the *Comet* that about four o'clock on Sunday afternoon, a strong breeze arose from the northeast. When the winds subsided about four hours later, the weather became very thick and foggy. The Captain ordered the vessel in a direction one point eastward of the usual route in order to avoid Cape Croker and Griffith Island.

A few minutes before ten o'clock at night, with the fog continuing to thicken, McGregor called the mate to consider a proper course of action. They decided that the vessel should stand off into

Georgian Bay until morning. Ironically, the moment the captain gave this order, the *Belle* collided with something. Not until the next morning did they discover that they had wrecked on Cape Croker, or, as it was also known, Cape Montresser. Fortunately, there were no casualties. While the *Belle* was valued at about $22,000, it was only insured for $14,000. The cost of repairs was estimated at about $5,000.[7]

The *Comet* reported that it was not known when another vessel would replace the *Belle*, but it would be at least two weeks, if not longer. This news, no doubt, caused many in the community to wonder about a potential shortage of supplies or how they might send their produce to market.

Shipping disasters and caution concerning the waters of Georgian Bay provided frequent entries for the Owen Sound newspapers. Reports of disaster meant many things to the citizens of pioneer settlement, as well as often meaning the loss of loved ones, friends and neighbours.

A few months after the *Belle's* catastrophic voyage another vessel sank. In its September 17, 1852 edition the *Comet* reported that the *Lily*, a ship owned and operated by Mr. Hartley from Penetanguishene, had wrecked on the rocks as it entered Tobermory harbour. The story illustrates the ordeal that many vessels endured as they attempted to navigate waterways of the region. The *Lily* entered the channel between Cove and Cat islands at night and struck a rock. Fortunately, the captain was able to get his ship off the rock and into an inlet on Cove Island for repairs. He then set out again on the voyage, only to have the winds die, "the dead swells carried him" onto "the rocks at the entrance of Tupper Murray (Tobermory) harbour effectively destroying the ship.[8]

In the same article, the editor of the *Comet* suggested that the incident might have been prevented. Apparently, the sunken rock in the ship channel had been marked on Bayfield's chart some fifteen years earlier. Bayfield, a British naval officer, led the expedition to map the Georgian Bay region shortly after the War of 1812. It was suggested that "...reference thereto may prevent damage hereafter."[9]

Repairing vessels which had been either sunk or damaged in some maritime accident was an ongoing occurrence. In September 1852, the newspaper announced that the brigantine *Sophia* recently wrecked at the mouth of the Nottawasaga River and was now safely moored in that river and being refitted. The report went on to say that the 103 ton

Sophia would be used to carry produce and passengers between Owen Sound and other Georgian Bay ports to and from Toronto.[10]

When the *Sophia* arrived in port the following June, it was important news in the local paper. The report gives an indication of the cargo and its consignees:

"This anxiously awaited vessel freighted with goods for Owen Sound alone, as near as we can ascertain from the Insurance Agent, to the amount of $10,000, hove in sight Tuesday afternoon, and dropped her anchor about 5 o'clock pm. Until now we had not had the pleasure of examining this fine vessel, which is fitted out in the very best style for appearance, comfort, convenience and capacity; with a second cabin. We observed on board boxes, bales & c. for the following parties:

A. Neelands—General Merchandise
John Frost
Christie and Corbet—Coal for Foundry
A.M. Stephens—Dry Goods & c.
Owen Vandusen—Printing Paper, Books and Stationery
P. Lenfesty—Goods & c.
R. Carney
F. LePan—Goods, Hard, Dry & c.
R. Hadden." [11]

Also on board were goods for businesses located in Meaford and Collingwood.

In 1853, the community was still without consistent and regular mail service. An event occurred in April of that year which illustrates the extreme competition between vessels to bring produce and passengers to the area, but due to this rivalry the mail sometimes suffered.

The *May Flower*, *Queen of the West*, *Magnet* and the *Princess Royal* all left Hamilton on the same morning. Although some vessels had stops to make at other ports along the route, they all arrived within a similar time frame. Because of the stiff competition for maritime commercial trade, the *Princess Royal* failed to call at either Oakville or Port Credit to pick up the mail that was bound for the Owen Sound region. When it was discovered that there would be no mail from the two

By the 1880s, the harbour area included grain elevators built by the CPR. The fleet of sailing vessels carried grain between Chicago and Owen Sound. In the foreground, the large ship is either the *Alberta* or the *Athabaska* of the CPR fleet. The barren undeveloped west bank of the Sydenham, where the elevators stand today, would not become more active until the arrival of the Grand Trunk Railway in the 1890s. *Courtesy Grey County Archives.*

centres that were bypassed for the sake of speed, the *Comet* suggested that it "...would be just as well that a check were put to this absurdity at its commencement."[12]

In 1851, a vessel arrived in Owen Sound's harbour carrying a passenger of some note or notoriety, depending upon political persuasion. Late one humid, summer Saturday, the steamer *Mohawk* arrived unannounced at Boyd's Wharf. Consequently there was no official party to welcome James Bruce, the eighth Earl of Elgin, the Governor General of Canada!

Earlier that year Lord Elgin had signed the unpopular Rebellion Losses Bill. To escape the rancour of Loyalists towards this unpopular legislation, which in effect indemnified the rebels for their rebellion losses, the Governor General had boarded the *Mohawk* to visit the hinterland of Upper Canada. Actually, Owen Sound had not been on Lord Elgin's itinerary, but the *Mohawk* needed more wood to fuel the next leg of the excursion. Besides the Governor General wanted to attend an Anglican church service.[13]

As news of the Governor General's arrival spread through town, a hastily assembled entourage led by Richard Carney, made its way to the wharf. After the presentation of gifts of trout and venison, Carney offered the use of an honour guard to keep sightseers and other visitors away from the wharf and the vessel. Lord Elgin inquired of the presence of an Anglican church and announced that he would be in attendance the following morning.[14]

The Anglican church,a building located on Poulett Street, was a tiny 18' x 24' rough-hewn log building that had been donated to the congregation as a place of worship by Thomas Hinchcliff, a prominent Anglican merchant.[15] News that the congregation would have vice-regal visitor the next morning ignited a flurry of activity in the church building. The church was cleaned and dusted. Fires were lit. Then, someone realized the building contained no chair suitable for a vice-regal visitor. Mrs. Hinchcliff solved the dilemma by offering "...a magnificent rush bottomed..."[16] chair she had brought with her from England.

As the "vice-regal" procession made its way to the tiny church the next morning, most of the citizens of the community lined its muddy streets to catch a glimpse of their distinguished visitor. Upon arrival, the entourage entered and the choir opened the service with a hymn. Those in attendance noted that Mr. Hinchcliff was absent. It would not be long, however, before the major benefactor of the Anglican church made his presence felt!

As Rev. (later Archdeacon) Mulholland delivered his sermon, a noise arose from outside the church. Suddenly, the door swung open! There stood an irate Mr. Hinchcliff! Incensed over Elgin's treatment of the French rebels, he hurled insults at the Governor General. Not wanting confrontation, Lord Elgin tried to remove himself from the church as politely and diplomatically as possible. He and his entourage got up and headed to their coach and back to the *Mohawk*.

Those also in attendance at the service also left, leaving an irate Hinchcliff to vent his rage. Author Andrew Armitage describes what happened next:

"The clamour and crashing inside the church grew louder. Out through the door came the plank pews, one by one skipping off the boardwalk and into the street. Hinchcliff appeared briefly, holding the pulpit high over his head. It splintered into pieces. Just as Lord Elgin and his aides were struggling for balance in the retreating wagon Hinchcliff appeared one last time.

Trembling with anger he held the rush-bottomed chair before him. Searching for support from the gaping crowd he yelled, "That man signed the bill to pay the rebels and now his traitorous arse has fouled my chair." Hinchcliff tore the chair to bits, hurling rungs and posts after the speeding wagon and white-faced passengers." [17]

The Governor General arrived at the *Mohawk* as her captain ordered the fires to be stoked. Apologies to Lord Elgin were made on behalf of the much embarassed community, and the vessel made its way out into Georgian Bay. Soon after the incident the Hinchcliff's sold their business and left town.

It would be another quarter of a century before Owen Sound hosted another vice-regal visit.

EARLY AFRICAN-AMERICAN
CITIZENS OF OWEN SOUND

I n the 1850s, the community of Owen Sound welcomed many more
new residents. Among these newcomers were African-Americans
who had escaped from slavery in the United States and made their
way to Canada via the "Underground Railway." Once slavery was
abolished in all parts of the British Empire in 1833, many made their
way as far north as Sydenham village. The extent of the number of former slaves who arrived in Owen Sound is hard to determine with any
exactitude, but the 1861 Census shows that 88 African-Americans
lived in the community. By the time of the 1880 Census, this number
had risen to 667.[1] Great Lakes historian James Barry suggests that at
one time ten percent of Owen Sound's population was African-American. [2] The history of this group of people in Owen Sound has hitherto been an area which has been neither well documented or
researched. Consequently, it is difficult to describe with a lot of cer-
tainty the events surrounding life in that community.

One of the debates is over who was the first African-American citizen
in Owen Sound. Some attribute this honour to John "Daddy" Hall, a
flamboyant character in and around town for more than half a century.
Still others claim that Thomas Henry Miller, Henry Cousby, Edward Patterson and Thomas Green who arrived in the settlement sometime
around 1851 should all be recognized as the first to arrive.[3] One thing is
certain, Mr. Miller holds the distinction of being the first minister at the
first British Methodist Episcopal Church in Owen Sound. [4]

Despite the fact that Owen Sound had as many as three newspapers to carry the news of the day and advisements, many companies employed the use of a Town Crier or Town Bell Ringer to announce their sales or other events. One of more popular Town Criers to work the streets of Owen Sound was John "Daddy" Hall. Arriving in Owen Sound in the 1850s, he certainly is one of the early African-American citizens of this community. He lived on the north end of Victoria Park which was then known as the Pleasure Grounds.

Each day, at about 10:00 in the morning, "Daddy" Hall would arrive at the corner of 10th Street and 3rd Avenue East and commence to announce the "news" of the day. He would ring his bell and announce his message. An example of the type of message that Hall would deliver was carried in an early edition of the *Sun Times*:

> "To whom it may concern: Be it known unto you and to all to whom you may deliver this message, that there will be sold on the market square in the Town of Owen Sound, by George James Gale, licensed auctioneer for the County of Grey, in the Province of Upper Canada, under and by virtue of power of sale, contained in a certain chattel mortgage which will be produced at the time of sale; namely six sheep and four lambs, two cows and one yoke of oxen. Terms—Cash. Remember the hour this afternoon at half-past two o'clock, on the Market Square. God Save the Queen."

After delivering his message, Hall would proceed to the corner of 10th Street and 2nd Avenue East. While he walked he would swing his bell over his shoulder and around in a circle. After making his announcement, Hall would then proceed in a similar fashion along 2nd Avenue East, stopping at the corner of 9th Street and then halfway between 8th and 9th Streets to once again call out his message. "Daddy" Hall would complete his route with a ringing message at the Market Square.

At 2:00 pm Hall would repeat this process, perhaps with the same message or a new one. The one constant in each of Hall's pronouncements was that he ended every message with "God Save the Queen."

This work must have agreed with Hall. He was a popular figure around town and was well liked by everyone. Working out of doors in all types of climate did not seem to impact on his health as he lived to be more than 100 years old. In fact, some claim that when he died on

April 11, 1900 he was 117 years old!

How "Daddy" Hall arrived in Owen Sound is an interesting story in itself. He claimed to have been a scout for Tecumseh in the War of 1812. But before the war was over he returned to his home near Amherstburg. Here, he and his family were captured by American troops and sold into slavery. Hall was sent to Kentucky to work on a plantation, but escaped and made his way back to Amherstburg. When he was unable to find his family he moved on to the Rocky Saugeen area north of Durham and eventually ended up in Owen Sound.

Research for this book has led to the awareness of another who might lay claim to being the first African-American resident of Owen Sound. Around 1841 to 1842, Isaiah Chokee arrived in the frontier settlement aboard the *Fly*,

One of the unidentified African-American residents of Owen Sound. *Courtesy County of Grey-Owen Sound Museum.*

a vessel owned by W. C. Boyd. Chokee worked as a cook and deck hand aboard Boyd's vessel. After Boyd sold his ship, evidence of Chokee's presence in the area disappears. However, it has been said that he may possibly have moved south of Owen Sound, probably to Holland or Glenelg townships.

Many historians report that Owen Sound became a popular destination for African-Americans, especially those seeking freedom from slavery. One of the first objectives of the members of the African-American community was to establish a place of worship. Some claim that John Frost, the prominent businessman and community leader in Owen Sound, provided his home as a place of worship for those African-Americans who first arrived. However, while this is acknowledged as being possible, there is no proof to substantiate the claim. It is known, however, that John Frost had a close supportive relationship with this community. In 1889, a book entitled *Broken Shackles* was published under the pseudonym of Glenelg. The author was John Frost; the story was based on Jim "Old Man" Henson's remembrances

The British Methodist Episcopal Church of Owen Sound, 1865–1911. The photograph was taken just before the church was demolished in 1993. *Courtesy Paula Niall Collection.*

from his time as a slave in Maryland to finally his freedom in Canada, in Owen Sound.

Many members of the African-American communtiy were very devout Christians and they continued to worship with the assistance of dedicated lay preachers. Angus McIntosh, a Free Church Presbyterian minister "conducted services in the homes of black families along the Garafraxa Road in 1844."[5] On September 29, 1856, the British Methodist Episcopal Church was established as an independent denomination. After at least three temporary locations, they moved into a permanent structure around 1865. This church, often referred to as "Little Zion," was a source of pride and strength for the community. Located north of 745 2nd Avenue West, it sat a short distance south of the current location of the library. The land was originally owned by Mr. Joseph Maugham and his wife, Mary. On July 24, 1865, they deeded a 25 foot by 40 foot section of their property to the trustees of the Owen Sound British Methodist Church. These trustees included James Henson, Thomas Miller, Isaac Wilson of Owen Sound and Samuel Barnes and John Edwards of nearby Derby township.

The frame structure had rounded windows and, probably because of a shortage of space, there was no parking lot for horse drawn vehicles. Abutting the sidewalk on 2nd Avenue West, the structure remained in that location until 1911 when the congregation purchased the former Westside Methodist Church on 11th Street West. This location still serves the spiritual needs of the community.

MEMORIAL

No. 11815–20

Maugham wife

to

Trustees of the

Owen Sound Coloured
Congregation of British
Episcopal Methodists

Recorded this 12th day
of October 1865 at 12 o'clock
a.m. in — —
— 264.26-266

Jas. Douglas, Registrar
A MEMORIAL for registration of a Deed of Sale in the words
following, that is to say,

"This indenture made this twenty fourth day of July in the
year of our Lord one thousand eight hundred and sixty-five,
Between *Joseph Maugham* of the town of Owen Sound in the
County of Grey and Province of Canada, Esquire; of the first
part; *Mary Hughes Maugham* of the same place, wife of the
same party of the first part; of the Second part. And *James Henson, Thomas Miller* and *Isaac Wilson* of Owen Sound aforesaid
Yoemen and *Samuel Barnes* and *John Edwards* of the Township
of Derby in this said County, Yoeman; Trustees of the Owen
Sound Coloured Congregation of the British Methodist Episcopal Church in Canada of the third part."

After the congregation moved to their current location, "Little
Zion" was sold sometime between 1911 and 1922 and moved to a spot

behind the home of T.I. Thomson at 781 2nd Avenue West where it was used as a garage.

Throughout the early years of settlement in Owen Sound, the African-American residents of the community eagerly looked forward to one date each year. That day was August 3 which was also known as Emancipation Day. Each year this community gathered together for song, worship and entertainment as they celebrated the anniversary of the official declaration by Britain which freed the slaves in the British West Indies.

In one undated article from an Owen Sound newspaper, an Emancipation Day celebration, organized by the British Methodist Church at nearby Presque Isle on the west shore of Owen Sound, is described. The celebrants traveled to Presque Isle on the steamer *Alderson* for a picnic. The African-American residents of the area were not the only ones to enjoy the celebrations that warm August day. Others who attended included W.P. Telford, Rev. Kerr and Rev. Holmes as well as other residents from Owen Sound and Presque Isle. Within the report, it was noted that James "Old Man" Henson, reputed to be about 100 years old at the time, was called upon to speak to those assembled.

Over the years, it appears that much of the history of the African-Americans has all but disappeared. It is hoped that with this renewed interest in this aspect of Owen Sound's emergence as a community, that the definitive story of these African-Americans will be told.

COMING OF AGE

I n 1856 Owen Sound incorporated as a town. In that same year, a new stone school was constructed large enough to accommodate students from the immediate community and beyond. In order to house young scholars who travelled from elsewhere in Grey and Bruce counties, some teachers pooled their resources to purchase and operate a boarding house on 3rd Avenue East. The Clifton House became home away from home for many students. During 1877–78, a young man named William Wilfred Campbell whose parents lived in Wiarton boarded at the Clifton House.[1] Later in life Campbell would achieve status as one of Canada's leading poets. The "Stone School" continued as both an elementary and secondary school until 1878 when it was deemed necessary to build facilities solely for the teaching of high school students.

The Stone School was not the first school house in Owen Sound. Some historians suggest that the first classes were held in the government building which John Telfer erected in 1840–41. In 1842, a school was built on what is now 24th Street West in the village of Newash. The next year, 1843, a formal school was established in the Land Agent's building.

School life in Owen Sound likely resembled that of other pioneering Ontario communities. Melba Croft in her book, *Fourth Entrance to Huronia*, relates some of the experiences of James Andrew who attended school here in 1849, notably a description of the rawhide whip used to enforce discipline in the classroom. But, even more telling is the revelation about drinking water quality in Owen Sound, generally considered quite questionable in taste and purity. Therefore, a hollowed log was placed at the school house door. Whiskey was poured into this vessel and a dipper stood at the ready to quench the thirst of the scholars![2]

Perhaps it was poor water quality or the early introduction of residents to alcohol, but the 1850s also marked the beginning of a long and troublesome relationship with alcoholic consumption in the community. During the 1850s, the *Comet* carried many articles about problems posed by alcohol. In the February 21, 1852 edition, it was reported that councillor and prominent businessman John Frost called for a limit on the number of tavern licenses, as already there were 70 taverns in nearby Simcoe County. As a result, a bylaw was drawn up to limit the number of taverns in Owen Sound to five.[3]

Alcohol was widely available. A bottle of whiskey sold for $1.00 a bottle. By the late 1850s, it was said that five hotels existed between Owen Sound and Allenford. The accepted practice for many men was to carry a bottle with them on their travels, if, however, one left his bottle at home or ran out of the elixir, the common price at taverns and inns was six drinks for a quarter, or two pence a glass. Many who did not drink but stopped at one of the inns, after resting a while, would leave a quarter on the bar before continuing their journey. This practice was probably due to an appreciation by the travellers for the hospitality of the innkeeper, in spite of the fact that no alcohol had been consumed.[4]

In 1854, W.C. Boyd, who headed the Total Abstinence Society, called a mass meeting of all citizens to discuss solutions to the problems posed by alcohol consumption and to consider the possibility of asking the government to enact legislation that would prohibit the manufacture and sale of liquor.[5]

Although the general community may have had a liberal attitude towards the consumption of alcohol, it strictly observed a prohibition against work on Sunday! Activities of just about any kind were frowned upon. The Sabbath law was strictly enforced even in the most desperate circumstances. This stringent attitude was demonstrated when a man arrived at the Inglis Mill late one Saturday evening. He told the miller, his family was without food until he could return with ground wheat. The sympathetic miller worked into the night and the early hours of Sunday morning to ensure that the man could return home with food for his family. As the man was returning home with the ground wheat, a citizen stopped and detained him somehow until Monday, according to the recollections of A.M. Stephens. His pleas to be allowed to go home to feed his family fell on deaf ears. On Monday, the man was charged, found guilty of transgressing the Sunday laws and fined. Only then was he allowed to return home with the flour to feed his family.

Perhaps the most ironic of known cases concerning the breaking of the Sabbath ordinance occurred in the mid-1850s. The priest in charge of the Owen Sound Catholic Parish had drowned and two young priests arrived from France to take up his duties. Both were avid outdoorsmen who must have been pleased with being assigned to an area which provided ample opportunity for fishing and hunting. One Sunday afternoon the two were seen hunting in the forest on the west side of Owen Sound. The person who saw them went directly to a magistrate in order to lay charges.

Fortunately for the young priests, the magistrate was sympathetic, understanding the naivety of the newcomers in terms of Upper Canadian laws. He visited them at their parish and, after explaining their transgression, accepted their apologies and promises never to break the Sabbath law again.[6]

It seems that the everyday citizens, along with the law enforcers and the law makers, frowned on many activities as unsuited to the religious day of rest. An 1855 County Council meeting noted that it was not only illegal to hunt and fish on Sundays but it was also against the law "...to play marbles, cricket, ball, skittles or any noisy game or to gamble with dice."[7]

The first reported legal case in the new community seemed to illustrate that decisions could be made even in the most primitive situations without having to rely upon a system of courts and lawyers. The event occurred when James Oliver was chopping down a tree. When the tree fell, it killed an ox owned by his neighbour, Edward Sparling. Although the unfortunate incident had been accidental, Oliver and Sparling were unable to agree upon compensation for the dead ox.

It was decided that both parties would make presentations to the land agent and to W. C. Boyd, and that their decision would be final. In order to come to a decision, the two men referred to "Exodus, Chapter 21, Verse 35."[8] They placed a value on the dead animal and deemed that Oliver should pay to Sparling half of that amount. Finally,

By the early 1900s, Poulett Street (renamed 2nd Avenue in 1909) presented a substantial business streetscape. The commerial signage is prominent. Note the barber pole and wooden sidewalks. It is believed that the name Poulett may have been in honour of Lord Sydenham, Charles Poulett Thompson. *Courtesy Grey County Archives.*

the carcass should be cut in half and shared between the two men. Stephens reported that both men agreed to these terms and "...went home good friends."[9]

During the 1850s, it was decided that the community was large enough to require a public cemetery. Consequently, a large plot of land, of about 40 acres in extent was designated for public burial purposes in 1854. In that year Greenwood Cemetery was opened. A mausoleum, with Indiana limestone on the outside and Italian marble on the inside, was erected on the site some years later in 1927. This impressive building also included a large chapel with several stained glass windows.

Despite a lack of the tools that make up a "civilized" community, the citizens of this small outpost managed to keep some semblance of order in their town. By the mid 1850s, even without effective transportation and communication links, Owen Sound was developing into a prosperous community full of anticipation for continued expansion.

13

INDUSTRIAL GROWTH

O wen Sound officially became a town in 1856. During the first decade and a half the community mushroomed from being a wilderness clearing to a town on the verge of yet further expansion. The port function had grown in pace with the emergence of a small core of businesses and industries. However, the one essential component which Owen Sound still lacked was a railroad connection with the rest of the colony.

During the next decade and a half, the community would experience both boom and bust. A severe economic downturn in 1859 would require Warden George Jackson to go to Toronto and appeal for government aid. (He received a grant of $10,000 and later, at the April 1859 session, Council authorized borrowing $20,000 for relief purposes.[1]) These events, however, did not deter the citizens from pursuing their goals of a railroad connection and an improved maritime commercial link. Anticipation of such developments provided the impetus to push growth and expansion in Owen Sound.

Despite the current lack of a railway connection with the markets of Southern Ontario, Owen Sound still experienced industrial and commercial growth in the 1850s. In 1856, William Kennedy, a thirty-five-year-old Scottish millwright from Smith Falls, arrived to install machinery in the Harrison Woollen and Grist Mills. This event marked the beginning of a long and fruitful relationship between the community and the Kennedy family.

Matthew Kennedy succeeded his father, Willliam, as head of the industrial enterprise known as Wm. Kennedy and Sons. Matthew became very active in Owen
Sound politics ultimately becoming mayor in 1885 and again in 1907. His home,
still standing today, is located in the centre of the 900 block of 1st Avenue West.
Courtesy County of Grey-Owen Sound Museum.

Like the other pioneers who established themselves in the Owen
Sound area, Kennedy realized that the region offered an opportunity
to improve his own lot in life. In 1857, he began a venture which would
have a great impact on Owen Sound for the next one and a half centuries! In that year Kennedy started a planing and matching mill. Due
to his drive, determination and skill, the business expanded and was
enormously successful. Six years later in 1863, because of an ever-
expanding market, Kennedy found it necessary to erect a large, two-
storey factory. One floor was dedicated to the sash and door business,
while the other floor housed a new machine shop.

Kennedy realized that Owen Sound was on the verge of becoming
a dynamic Great Lakes port. In order to meet the needs of this perceived market, the ambitious Scotsman added a new facet to his
already booming enterprise. He began manufacturing equipment for
fishing, passenger, freight and pleasure vessels.

In 1867, in the year of Confederation, following the expansion of
the original Kennedy Planing and Matching Mill, William Kennedy re-
named his company Wm. Kennedy and Sons. Throughout the next 25

years, Kennedy expanded his operations to include the manufacture of machinery for saw, grist and flour mills. By the end of 1884, the company had moved from its location by the mill dam to First Avenue West, near the Corbet Machine Shop which had been established on First Avenue West by George Corbet and his four sons in 1851.

William Kennedy died in 1885, at the age of 64. However, this did not mean an end to the Kennedy dynasty as Matthew Kennedy took over his father's business.

Possessing similar entrepreneurial drive and determination, the younger Kennedy continued in his father's footsteps. Also keenly interested in the development of his community, Matthew served for several years on the town council and on two occasions, 1885 to 1886 and 1907 to 1908, was elected to the position of mayor. In 1899, he set up a steel foundry. By 1911, Wm. Kennedy and Sons had grown from an essentially, one-man operation to employ 150 area residents in the manufacture of such products as turbines, mill gearings, steel castings and propellers. With the onset of World War I, Kennedys became important contributers to the allied war effort. The March 2, 1915 edition of the Owen Sound *Times* reported that the company had received an order to manufacture 25,000 shells for the Canadian army.

The Kennedy operation continued to expand. In 1916, Matthew Kennedy bought and merged the Owen Sound Iron Works into his operations. Three years later, he purchased the Canadian Malleable Iron Works located on the east shore of Owen Sound's harbour. Expansion during the 1920s helped the company survive the Depression which swept North America, forcing many other companies to close.

The Second World War saw the company fortunes boom. The foundry produced propellers for the Canadian Merchant Marine as well as for merchant vessels in countries such as China and Brazil. Most naval vessels used by the Allied forces had propellers manufactured in Owen Sound.

In 1951, almost a century after William Kennedy had begun his pioneering venture in the small community of Owen Sound, the company was sold to Had-Mil (Canada) Limited, a division of the Sheffield, England, Millspaugh Corporation. A decade later the company was once again sold, the new owner being Black Clawson Ltd., an Ohio-based company.

Today, due to corporate "down-sizing" and "contracting-out," the company which once employed hundreds of Owen Sounders, has ceased operations. The once mighty foundry furnaces on the banks of

John Harrison and family, 1871. Front (l to r): Mrs. John Harrison (nee Emma Rachel Hart (1841-1915); James Edward Harrison (b. 1880); Frederick William Harrison (1863-1915), served as Mayor of Owen Sound circa 1909; John Harrison (1824-1902).Back (l to r): Rachel (b. 1876) Ephrehan John Harrison (b. 1873); Arthur Nathan Harrison (b. 1873); May Emma Harrison (b. 1877). *Courtesy County of Grey-Owen Sound Museum.*

the Sydenham River lie silent, an obvious reminder of an era when the clang of metal being forged for customers all over the world could be heard twenty-four hours a day.

When William Kennedy first arrived, the Owen Sound company which had contracted his services, Harrison Mills, had been operating in the area for almost a decade. The Harrison family would continue to provide major industrial employment in Owen Sound well into the next century.

In March 1848, William Harrison Jr., his young family and his brother Robert, arrived in the community of Sydenham from Wellington County. The brothers built a house on what is now 3rd Avenue East, between 10th and 11th Streets. Shortly after their arrival they were joined by another brother, John.[2]

Anxious to begin a new life, the brothers bought, from James Frost,[3] a sawmill and grist mill set on a plot of land near the present location of the mill dam.

John took charge of the sawmill operation and earned a reputation as a determined hard worker. Anecdotes survive of John going into the forest and felling a tree, then dragging it to the mill and cutting it into lumber without any assistance!

Robert managed the grist mill and, for a time, carded wool on the building's second floor. Before long, a separate woollen mill was erected on the site and William took charge of its operation; and, in 1857, the brothers added the Harrison Flour Mills to their enterprise on the same site as their other mills.[4]

Tragedy struck the Harrison family in 1866. Robert, a member of the 31st Regiment, was called to active service with the outbreak of the Fenian Raids. He served in the Lake Erie region and, when discharged, returned to his father's home in Puslinch, seriously ill. There he died in 1866.

Shortly after Robert's death the business was sold in order to straighten out his estate. At the auction, William purchased both of his other brother's shares in the woollen and grist mill business. Unfortunately, thirteen years later, William passed away. However, the Harrison Woollen and Grist Mill was maintained for many years by William's widow and sons. The mill was finally sold to the Northern Textile Company in 1927.[5]

The death of his brother Robert had a great impact on John Harrison. After the sale of the business to William, he seems to have been unsure of what the future held in store for him.

One day, while hunting and fishing in the marshes at the mouth of Sydenham River, he was struck with an idea which would lead him on a new entrepreneurial adventure. Harrison decided to erect a steam-driven sawmill at the mouth of that river.

John Harrison was a man of considerable strength and will-power. When he needed leather for his first mill, he walked to Guelph, purchased the leather necessary for the heavy belts, loaded them on to a hand sleigh and walked back to Owen Sound, pulling the sleigh behind him!

A further indication of John Harrison's strength and determination occurred when he discovered a tumour in his back. Again, he walked to Guelph to have a doctor examine the growth and sat straddling a chair while the doctor cut the tumour out. Later, he walked back to Owen Sound!

In 1869 John erected his new mill, but, in 1875, he was forced to rebuild his operation when fire destroyed the original mill. Once again

Harrison Park as represented in a watercolour by Flora Robinson, 1920. The Inn
(centre left) was destroyed by fire. Today a modern restaurant stands in its place.
Courtesy County of Grey-Owen Sound Museum.

in 1887, fire ravaged the sawmill and necessitated the building of yet
another.[6] To ensure a supply of timber for his operations, John bought
farm lots in the Allenford area and, later, operated lumber camps in
more northerly areas of the Bruce Peninsula and some of the islands
located in northern Georgian Bay.

In 1875, John and Emma Harrison purchased part of Lots 13 and
14, Concession 1 and part of Lot 14 on Concession 2 in Derby township from the estate of John Frost. The entire land package, adjacent
to the Owen Sound town boundary, was purchased for $3,100. About
80 acres was designated to become parkland. Part of Lot 1, 1st Range
west of the river was acquired by John Harrison in 1893, enabling him
to improve the entrance way to the Park. By 1912, the park was valued at $10,000, but Harrison offered it to the city for $5,000, an offer
that was accepted. In recognition of the generosity and civic minded-
ness of the Harrison family, this park along the Sydenham River is
known as Harrison Park. To this day, it remains a valued recreation
landmark for tourists and local citizens.

It may come as a surprise to citizens of Owen Sound that the original industrial sector of this community was around the location of the
mill dam. Today this is a quiet residential section, but, in Owen Sound's
first few decades it was the heart of the community's industry, the site
chosen for the ready availability of water power to run the mills.

In 1862, the Chatwin and Commedy Cabinet Factory joined
Kennedy and the Harrisons on the banks of the Sydenham near the

View from the south of the Mill Dam area, circa 1872. Today the land shown below the river is known as "Millionaire's Drive." *Courtesy County of Grey-Owen Sound Museum.*

mill dam. Quinn's tannery, established in 1857, had as its defined location the south end of 2nd Avenue East, close to other industrial sites.

Another manufacturing business with a unique product would commence operations in Owen Sound in 1856. John Sloane established a factory to manufacture melodeons, a musical insrument defined as "...a small reed organ in which air is sucked inward by a bellows, an American predecessor of the harmonium."[8] It is hard to imagine why someone would manufacture such instruments in what was still very much an isolated area! Even so, Sloan must have made a quality product and been a successful salesman. He continued at his vocation until his death in 1892.

Considering the lack of efficient transportation links with the rest of the Upper Canadian colony and the world beyond, the success of Kennedy, the Harrisons and others further illustrates the desire and determination of these early settlers of Owen Sound.

14

THE GROWTH OF THE HARBOUR

Despite the lack of a direct railway connection and the economic decline around 1859, business in Owen Sound's harbour continued to grow throughout the 1850s and 1860s.

In Owen Sound's first decade the lake vessels were small, and only a few of them used steam power. "The largest of the boats would not be more than 125 feet on the keel, with a maximum of 30 foot beam."[1] Gradually, however, the masted sailing vessels gave way to steam. The first steamer to enter service in this area was the *Gore*. While the smaller vessels had little trouble entering Owen Sound's harbour, as vessels became larger and carried more weight the water levels of the harbour became a concern for those who wanted to increase marine transportation.

The *Gore* weighed 189 tons. As larger vessels, such as the *Kalloola* weighing 250 tons, entered service on Georgian Bay, there was danger that Owen Sound might fall by the wayside in competition with other ports. This potential, combined with the fact that there was no rail connection, would spell doom for industries established here, and therefore limit any potential future growth.

By 1856, a line of steamers regularly plied the waters between Chicago and Collingwood, but Owen Sound's connection with these vessels was sporadic at best. Instead, a regular service between Collingwood and Owen Sound was attempted. In 1855, Captain W.W. Smith bought the *Oxford*, a paddle steamer with only a ninety foot keel, and put it into service between the two communities. Captain Butterworth sailed the steamer *Mazeppa* from Collingwood on alternate days to Smith's vessel. This service, however, proved unprofitable for both seamen and, in 1856, the *Oxford* was replaced by a larger and faster steamer, the *Canadian*, and Butterworth put his vessel into service on Lake Huron. For the next four years, Smith's *Canadian* provided the main service between Owen Sound and Collingwood. In 1860 the *Canadian* was replaced by the *Clifton*, Smith's newest vessel.[2]

In the early 1860s, an event occurred in the Owen Sound harbour which once again illustrated the tenacity and ingenuity of those Owen Sounders determined to improve their community's opportunity for growth. The sandbar across the mouth of the Sydenham River was effectively acting as a barrier to most vessels attempting to enter the harbour. Business and community leaders, concerned about the negative impact of this sandy barrier, petitioned the government to dredge the harbour. The government responded that only navigable waterways were eligible for dredging projects.

At this juncture, Captain Smith decided to take matters into his own hands. He stripped the *Clifton* of practically all her equipment, took the furniture from her cabin and had the water pumped from her boilers. The captain stood on the hurricane deck and gave orders to crew members aboard one of the vessel's life boats to carry the *Clifton's* anchors across the sandbar and drop them. The weight of the anchors pulled the vessel over the sandbar and into the river, thus "proving" the entrance to the harbour was navigable![3] Soon after the government authorized the dredging of Owen Sound's harbour.

Captain Smith retired the *Clifton* at the end of the 1866 sailing season. However, part of the vessel which saved maritime commerce in Owen Sound, would continue in service to her community. Smith installed the ship's machinery on the *Frances Smith*, a 182 foot paddle steamer built in Owen Sound. The largest vessel ever built to date on Georgian Bay,[4] the *Frances Smith* was described as "...the finest passenger steamer in her time on the upper lakes."[5]

Like the *Clifton*, the *Frances Smith* cruised between Collingwood and Owen Sound. She continued this route until the railway arrived in Owen Sound in 1873, at which point she went into service on a route connecting Collingwood, Owen Sound and Port Arthur on Lake Superior.

In 1870, the *Frances Smith*, took part in an historic mission. This vessel, along with the *Chicora* and the *Algoma* carried Colonel Garnet

In her time, the *Frances Smith* was the largest ship ever built on Georgian Bay.
Courtesy County of Grey-Owen Sound Museum.

Wolseley and his troops to Thunder Bay, from which point they marched to Manitoba to attempt to quell the first Riel Rebellion.[6]

To accommodate ships and their cargoes, the harbour wharfage and storage buildings became extremely important. In 1865, Owen Sound boasted such structures on both sides of the harbour. At the foot of 11th Street East, Captain Smith owned the Peel Warehouse, which was the first in the community to be outfitted with elevators. On the same side of the harbour, Thomas Maitland operated a warehouse, elevators and a wharf. Also on the east side of the harbour, was Rogerson and Ormiston's stone warehouse and wharf, while further up the harbour, George Spencer operated a lumberyard. On the west side, John Chisholm had a storage house, elevators and a wharf, and James Sutherland owned a storage building and a wharf.[7]

Despite obstacles incurred by the lack of a railway connection Owen Sound continued to thrive. Until the *Clifton* was retired Captain Smith's vessel made almost daily trips to Collingwood. The *Algoma* with Captain Leach at the helm made weekly excursions to Bruce Mines on the North Shore. There were also frequent visits by vessels from American ports such as Detroit and Chicago. While these maritime connections were seasonal, stagecoaches provided year-round connections from Guelph, Collingwood and Southampton.

By 1865, Owen Sound, now with about 2,500 citizens, [8] had at least twenty industrial enterprises. They included: Harrison's Flour Mills, Harrison's Sawmill, Harrison's Carding and Fulling Mill, Chatwin's Cabinet Factory, Ridell and Secord Brewery, Rositer's Fanning Mill; Quinn's Tannery, Lenfesty's Pearlash Mill, Boyd's Wharf, Owen Sound Iron Works, Frost's Tannery, Sloane's Melodian Factory, Crawford's Tannery, Frost Potash Works, Grey Foundry, Sydenham Foundry, Spencer's Cabinet Factory, Malone's Brewery, Dowsley's Carriage Works and Miller's Carriage Factory.[9] One has to wonder how much more well-developed Owen Sound might have been had there been a railroad connection in place!

15

FROM "PANIC" TO ANTICIPATION

In the mid-1860s fear of invasion swept the Canadian colony. The threat of raids by Fenians from the United States put all of Upper Canada on alert. The Owen Sound and Meaford militia companies were ordered to Sarnia to protect that border community. In Owen Sound the concern that boats carrying Fenian raiders might attack caused contingency plans to be put in order.

It was decided that women and children would take their families' valuables and retreat to caves on the escarpment west of town.[1] Meanwhile men and older boys, along with militia from other area communities, would defend the port.

As a result of this fear of the Fenians, an interesting event occurred one Sunday morning in April 1866. It all started in the Leith Presbyterian Church. As the minister was conducting the service, a messenger appeared. Quietly, he approached a member of the congregation and whispered a message into his ear. The parishioner went to the front of the church and whispered a message to the Reverend Alexander Hunter. The minister announced that a fleet of Fenian ships had been spotted off Griffith Island!

The result was immediate pandemonium. The members of the Leith Militia mustered and marched bravely to Owen Sound. Meanwhile the rest of the community of Leith went to the shore of Georgian Bay and watched the vessels manoeuvring on the far side of the bay. All day the citizens watched the boats while the militia and the men of Owen

Sound awaited nervously for the expected attack. As the sun dipped behind the escarpment all was quiet. The next morning the anxiety of all involved swept away and left a likely feeling of foolishness among some defenders and observers. The flotilla had been nothing more than a few fishermen, perhaps from Cape Croker, partaking in a regatta![2]

Once the Fenian threat dispersed, life returned to normal and in Owen Sound, the dream of a railway connection and the continued growth of the community re-emerged as the paramount goal. On a wider scale, the Canadian colony headed into preparations for Confederation in 1867.

In the year which would mark Canada's birth as a country, the first elections to select members of a national Parliament were held. Owen Sound's riding was the vast area known as the Algoma District. Two men, William Beatty of Parry Sound and Wemyss MacKenzie (W.M.) Simpson of Owen Sound, were the contestants.

Once again, the reliance upon sailing vessels for communications and transportation during that era would be illuminated. The only polling station for the election in Algoma was located in Sault Ste. Marie!

As election day approached, the two rivals chartered steamers to carry their supporters to Sault Ste. Marie to cast their ballots. Simpson and his entourage boarded the *Algoma*, while Beatty and his supporters sailed on the *Waubuno*. Unfortunately for Beatty, his vessel was delayed because of engine troubles and did not arrive in Sault Ste. Marie until after the polls had closed. Despite this turn of events, Simpson narrowly defeated Beatty by the slimmest margin, just nine votes![3]

Communications, however, were about to improve. In 1868, Owen Sound was connected with the rest of the province through its first telegraph system, established under the ownership of Edward Todd.[4] Although this innovation provided a direct communication link with the world beyond Owen Sound, it was not the solution to the community's economic needs. That dream, a line of steel, was still half a decade away.

The following year, an event on nearby White Cloud Island caused panic to grip the citizens of Owen Sound and the surrounding area. Captain Charles Fothergill, after buying provisions and withdrawing a substantial amount of money ($2,000.00) from the bank, left Owen Sound aboard his small boat. Owen Sound's postmaster, George Brown, along with Charles Kennedy and John Robinson, a recently arrived Civil War veteran, had been invited to sail with him to Colpoys Bay.

When Fothergill's vessel failed to arrive in Wiarton, a search party was sent to find him. The rescue party found the sailboat on the shore of White Cloud Island, its cargo still intact. Brown's dog was near the boat, but no passengers. Nearby, was the body of Kennedy. A search of the area turned up Fothergill's pocketbook, empty.

Although many other search parties scoured the islands and the shoreline of the area, the other three men were never found. Thirty years after the tragic event, campers on Griffith Island discovered three skeletons, but identification was not possible. To this day the fate of these individuals remains a mystery.[5]

On a happier note, the Victoria Skating Rink was erected on what is now the corner of 10th Street and 3rd Avenue East in 1869.[6] This event marked the beginning of a series of arenas which would provide hours of skating pleasure for the citizens of the area. Within two short decades, Owen Sound would enter the world of hockey competitions.

A month prior to the opening of the rink in November, the town of Owen Sound was once again gripped with "railway fever." On October 5, 1869, the first sod was turned at Weston to mark the beginning of construction of a rail line from Toronto to Orangeville.[7] However, it would take three more years before the first locomotive would steam into Owen Sound. Nonetheless, there seems to have been a sense within the community that, at last, their long awaited dream was about to become reality!

16

THE STRENGTHENING OF CIVIC PRIDE

After three decades of waiting, with the imminent arrival of the railway about to become a reality, the community anticipated ever more growth and development. But, both existing municipal offices and the marketplace were felt to be inadequate, not capable of meeting the needs of an expected prosperous future.

On March 23, 1868, a bylaw was passed for the drawing of a $10,000 debenture and plans were approved for the erection of a town hall facility which included a market building. There was some debate about erecting a clock tower as part of the complex. However, due to financial constraints it was finally decided that a tower would be built but with only a "dummy" clock.[1] While not entirely satisfactory, this compromise solution was agreed upon with the expectation that, at a later date when the tight financial constraints were alleviated, the "dummy" clock could be replaced.

The original contract was let for the sum of $14,500. While the Town Hall was completed in 1870, this project, unfortunately, was not completed without problems. The contractors ran out of money before the roof had been built. John P. Coulson, the owner of the Coulson House, stepped in and financed the rest of the construction. Coulson's support of the project cost him about $8,000 as the final calculations put the total cost of the Town Hall at about $22,500.[2]

Stores and market stalls occupied the main level of the complex and the south wing was rented to Molson's Bank for an annual sum of two hundred dollars.[3]

The "Dummy" Clock. When the Town Hall was built, officials decided to save money by installing a fake clock. Fifty years later, in 1920, to celebrate becoming a city, Owen Sound installed a real clock in the tower. *Courtesy County of Grey-Owen Sound Museum.*

It was not until Owen Sound received its designation as a city in 1920 that the "dummy" clock was replaced with a working fixture. It cost Owen Sound $3,112 to purchase the clock from the British firm, Gillet and Johnston, and another $6,000 to erect an appropriate tower.[4] This expense was probably justified by the community's leaders as the commemoration of Owen Sound's achieving the formal status of "city."[5]

Owen Sound's Town Hall, or City Hall as it is known today, has always been located almost directly on the location of John Telfer and Charles Rankin's historic first meeting on October 7, 1840.

Until the late 1880s, the community's fire department was located in the town hall complex. The origin of the fire department can be traced to the 1850s when the community purchased fire buckets and appointed citizens to act as volunteer fire fighters. In 1878, the community purchased a new fire bell from a manufacturer in Troy, New York. Nine years later, the department moved from the Town Hall to a building located next door on the main street of Owen Sound and remained in this location until 1974.

In the late 1800s, community fire departments were often sponsored by insurance companies and the Owen Sound fire department was not an exception to this rule. At first it was called the Owen Sound Victoria Fire Company, but in the 1890s sponsorship must have changed as a whole new name appeared on the scene, the Excelsior Fire Department.

Fire fighting was most important to communities during this era. Most buildings were still being constructed of wood and, with the increasing mechanization of industry, a volatile fire potential was ever present. Newspapers, periodicals and diaries from this era reveal the havoc created by fire.

One of the most catastrophic fires in Owen Sound occured on January 31, 1899, at the North American Bent Chair Company. When a company watchman sounded the alarm, the response of crews from the CPR and Grand Trunk railways was almost immediate. However, by the time the local volunteer firemen arrived on the scene with their equipment, an hour had elapsed. Once the fire-fighting equipment was finally in place, most of the efforts were directed at blocking the flames from spreading to other nearby businesses.[6]

Along with the Coulson House, J.P. Coulson owned hotels in Guelph and Meaford. As well, he owned a stage and freight line which operated between Owen Sound and Guelph. *Courtesy County of Grey-Owen Sound Museum.*

The entire Bent Chair complex was destroyed leaving 250 employees out of work. The fire caused more than $100,000 in damage and, unfortunately, only about one-quarter of that amount was covered by insurance. Despite the loss, within a year of the fire, company owners John and Archie Hay had erected a much larger, three storey complex on the site of their former enterprise.[7]

There had been many other fires during that period. The enormity of the overall impact of the fire, however, not only on the North American Bent Chair Company, but on the entire industrial complex nearby, caused many community leaders to consider improvements in fire protection. After much deliberation, the town enacted a bylaw creating the Owen Sound Fire Department in 1907. Although many fire fighters were still volunteers, this bylaw provided for the hiring of paid firemen. These salaried men were required to live at the fire hall seven days a week, and were on call 23 hours a day. Fire boxes were installed at various locations around Owen Sound. When activated, these boxes would ring in both the fire hall and the homes of volunteers.

The department used horses from the town's works' department to pull the steam pumper and a hose wagon. If these horses could not be located quickly, then horses were "borrowed" from the nearby market square. Finally, in 1903 the fire department purchased its own horses. "Jim" and "Jack" were the first of many horses to serve the department until 1939 when motorized vehicles took over.

The department established a unique system for the speedy harnessing of their horses. The harnesses were rigged immediately above

Ruins of the North American Bent Chair Factory destroyed by fire in 1899.
Courtesy County of Grey-Owen Sound Museum.

the horses in their stalls in such a way that they then could be dropped into place, directly on the horses below. All that was required was the tightening of a few straps and the fastening of buckles.

Today, Owen Sound boasts a fire department with state-of-the-art fighting equipment. The force is trained not only to fight fires in the traditional sense, but is also well-trained in the area of marine rescue. As well, Owen Sound is home of not one, but two fire stations. The community also hosts the Inter-Township Fire Department which serves the needs of the rural municipalities which surround the city. The presence of two well-equipped centres ensures that the community will never, it is hoped, suffer again the incredible losses that resulted from the devastating fires of earlier years.

At Last! A Line of Steel!

An omen of coming change occurred at 1:00 am, April 26, 1871,[1] when the citizens of the Owen Sound region were awakened to the rumbling of an earthquake. Fortunately, no one was injured, but the earthquake was, perhaps, symbolic of the shaking up that the community would undergo in the decade of the 1870s.

Although the town had progressed and expanded despite the lack of a railway connection with the rest of the province, this decade would mark the arrival of a ribbon of steel from Toronto. Led by a dynamic group of political and commercial leaders, the town would experience further growth and innovations, all of which suggested it was the ideal location for the CPR's eastern terminus for its Great Lakes fleet.

On June 12, 1873 there was another rumbling heard in Owen Sound. Only this time it was not an earthquake; it was the sound of the flower and flag festooned steam engine, the "Owen Sound," as she pulled the first train into the community. For this inaugural trial run, the train consisted of an engine, one truck, one baggage car and one passenger car.[2] The first regularly scheduled train between Toronto and Owen Sound would arrive on August 9, 1873.

This test trip took several hours longer than the regular train service would require. At each community along the route, the directors of the Toronto, Grey and Bruce Railway who were on board, were met by throngs of eager citizens excited about the prosperity that was sure to follow the ribbon of steel. All along the route, speeches made by

The narrow gauge locomotive engine "Caledon" was a familiar sight from the mid-to-late 1870s. *Courtesy County of Grey-Owen Sound Museum.*

local civic leaders expressed the appreciation felt towards the company for building the long-sought rail line. At Owen Sound the celebrations were on a grand scale! A memorial presented by town council and the local Board of Trade to the railway directors illustrated the vision of the expected prosperity.[3]

What did the arrival of the railroad actually mean? It provided a direct year round transportation connection with the rest of Ontario. No longer would producers have to store their grain and other goods for the winter until the first ships arrived in the spring. Although goods could be sent to Collingwood for transshipment out of the area, this was a very costly venture as a March 1871 letter to the editor of the Owen Sound *Advertiser* reveals when a local lumberman, Alex Fraser wrote:

Locomotive "721," one of the two engines used on the Toronto to Owen Sound Line. *Courtesy County of Grey-Owen Sound Museum.*

"[I] now have in Owen Sound over $5,000 of pine, oak and elm, which I have to raft to Collingwood, then to Toronto by [the] Northern Railway, raft again to Quebec. A direct line from Owen Sound would save me in this one small transaction, $500."[4]

A view of downtown Owen Sound, circa 1870. *Courtesy County of Grey-Owen Sound Museum.*

Most expected the railway connection would promote Owen Sound's port facilities even more. Even though there had been no previous rail link, Owen Sound had become a regular port of call for vessels plying the Great Lakes. By the 1870s, regularly scheduled routes existed between Georgian Bay ports and harbours on both Lake Superior and Lake Michigan. One such route ran between Chicago and Collingwood with a stopover in Owen Sound. It was hoped that this new rail connection would encourage vessels to direct more of their business to Owen Sound instead of Collingwood. A trip between Owen Sound and the mid-western ports would be faster and cheaper than a voyage that included a stop here and then continued on to Collingwood.

The arrival of the train also signalled the beginning of a new era for the community's commercial establishments. A broader range of merchandise at lower prices were now more readily available to local consumers.

Things appeared in stores in town, never seen before! Fashions for all the important functions could be brought by train from Toronto, if not readily accessible here. A major effect on dress shops resulted, with plate glass windows and window displays becoming more prevalent.[5]

THE "CORKSCREW" TOWN

The decade that followed the railway's arrival brought many innovations and changes to Owen Sound. Rail-related growth not only created new commercial enterprises, it also increased population. Consequently, improved services were required to meet the needs of a larger community. As well, social issues which had been brewing in the community now moved beyond tolerance, causing many to consider some sort of remedial action.

Problems related to alcohol had long been on the agenda of many concerned citizens in the community. By the mid 1870s, Owen Sound had received the moniker of "the corkscrew town."[1] During this decade some steps were taken to halt what many considered to be the excessive use of alcohol. To prove that one could enjoy a meal without alcohol, Donald Denoon, a prominent member of the community's prohibitionist movement, opened the Royal Saloon. Denoon's menu offered "all kinds of Temperance drinks; fish and oysters."[2]

In 1874, Mrs. R.J. [Mary Stephens] Doyle called upon all the women of the local area to attend a meeting to discuss taking action against what she considered the flagrant abuse of alcohol in the community. She contended that alcohol led to tragedy and poverty in the family and therefore its sale needed to be stopped. Owen Sound's reputation was so widely known that R.E. Spence writing in 1919 described Owen Sound of the 1870s as a "lake port town of between three and four thousand population, noted from Halifax to Vancouver for drunkenness and gambling."[3] At this meeting the Women's Prohibition Society was established. This group decided to circulate a petition asking for a halt to the issuing of any more saloon licenses, and that the Ontario Government amend the License Act.[4]

Another result of this meeting was the evolution of a new organization to combat the excessive use of alcohol. In 1874, the Women's Christian Temperance Union had been formed in Cleveland, Ohio. In the same year, the first Canadian branch of this organization was created in Owen Sound.[5] Although there was a vocal contingent of citizens who wanted the liquor problem solved by some form of prohibition, it would take another three decades before they successfully reached this goal. In 1903, with the "demon

Mrs. R.J. Doyle (Mary Stephens) and her sisters. Front (l-r): Rachel (Mrs. John Layton), Mary; back (l-r): Ellen (Mrs. David Layton), Eliza (Mrs. George S. Miller), circa 1890s. *Courtesy County of Grey-Owen Sound Museum.*

rum" still plaguing many citizens in Owen Sound, an organization called the Law and Order League was formed to fight against what was considered the rampant abuse of alcohol in the community. There were no controls on the 13 licensed saloons in the town which did not have closing hours and served already intoxicated patrons.

In 1905, an opportunity opened for the prohibitionists when the provincial government included a local option clause in the Liquor Licence Act. This action enabled municipalities to hold plebiscites concerning whether alcohol could be sold within the boundaries of the community. The response in Owen Sound was swift. The following January the town voted in favour of prohibition by a majority of 476 votes and, as if to reaffirm the position, seven councillors who stood on the prohibition platform were elected to the town council.

These stalwart men patrolled the streets of Owen Sound between 1908 and 1911 when Owen Sound was still a rowdy seaport. The Owen Sound Police Force: standing (l-r) A. Shute, J. McCauley, T.H. Carson; seated (l-r) W.O. Foster, J. Thompson. *Courtesy County of Grey-Owen Sound Museum.*

Owen Sound's nickname was changed from the "Corkscrew" town to "Dry Gulch" or "Sahara City." It would be not until 1961 that the Brewers' Retail and LCBO outlets were allowed to open in the city. It would take another twelve years before citizens were allowed to slake their thirst with an alcoholic beverage in a public place. In 1973, the town finally lost its reputation as the last "dry" city in Canada when the "wets," after six decades and six plebiscites finally defeated the "drys."

In 1879, perhaps in recognition of the significant maritime traffic between the port of Owen Sound and American destinations, the United States government established a trade consulate[6] in this community. However, some historians suggest that the real reason for the presence of a trade consulate related directly to the rowdy lifestyle in some quarters of Owen Sound. They maintain that the consulate's main function was to bail sailors out of the local jail to enable the ships to sail on schedule. The truth is difficult to ascertain. However, the story serves to confirm some of the complaints made by the temperance community of that era.

The abuse of alcohol was not the only source of derogatory names for Owen Sound. In 1874, Owen Sound earned itself the dubious title of "The Counterfeit Capital of Canada." An editorial in the *Advertiser* stated that "...for the last twenty years this town has been more or less the centre of counterfeiting, that people who lived here so long ago were engaged in this illegal practice, and it has continued down to the present time."[7] By early 1874, counterfeiting reached proportions which could no longer be tolerated. "A flood of 'plug nickels,' counterfeit coin of all denominations were duping the unwary all over town."[8]

Although the community's leaders were outraged at these events, it seemed that little action was being taken to quell the flow of "funny money." Because counterfeiting had been part of the area for so long, there were whispers that perhaps "...among the town's finest folks, a few bad 'yeggs' were to be found. Maybe, even the source of the counterfeit coin of the realm!"[9]

The seemingly ineffective official action prompted the editors of the local newspapers to take out their pens and mount their own crusade. The words of these journalists soon drew the attention of Oliver Mowat, the Ontario Attorney General. He sent undercover detectives to Owen Sound to determine the source of the counterfeit money. Either the townspeople were hiding something or the criminals were truly professional! The deputies returned to Toronto empty handed! Mowat's answer to the dilemma was to call John W. Murray, the self-proclaimed "Great Detective."[10]

Murray immediately headed to Owen Sound. The detective bragged that he always got his man and this case would be no exception. Within a short time he had not only located but had won the confidence of the criminals. Shortly thereafter he arrested and gained convictions of the four counterfeiters named Bentley, Taylor, McArthur, and Wilson.[11]

Although the men were in jail and their plates confiscated, John W. Murray was not through with the case. The "Great Detective" prided himself in the fact that he never let anyone get away. When the arrests had been made, the leader of the gang of counterfeiters, John C. Bond, had escaped. During the next year, the fact that Bond had eluded him haunted Murray. He sent posters to police detectives around the world, and everywhere he travelled he left money with police officers to bribe informants about the whereabouts of Bond.

Murray got his big break in the case when he tracked down Bond's brother in Lindsay, Ontario. There he learned there was a possibility that his man was in Evanston, Illinois! Murray immediately departed for that mid-west American city and arrested Bond. Despite his arrest, the counterfeit chief was seemingly not too concerned at first, according to Murray's recollection, Bond told Murray that it would be "...a mighty difficult task to convict a man in Owen Sound who had money and friends there."[12] However, the "Great Detective" had a surprise in store for him. The train they boarded went to Toronto, and not to Owen Sound! Bond was tried, convicted and sentenced to seven years in the Kingston Penitentiary.[13]

Fortunately, in spite of all of this noteriety, Owen Sound was also receiving positive attention through the visits of two distinguished men. In 1877, the community learned that Sir John A. Macdonald would visit Owen Sound on October 5 of that year. This was probably his first visit to the area since his near disastrous voyage on the *Ploughboy*, on Georgian Bay off the coast of the Bruce Peninsula, almost twenty years earlier. In July 1859 this sidewheel steamer had been commissioned for the use of the Premier of Upper Canada, John A. Macdonald, his cabinet and some prominent political supporters. Upon the arrival of their train in Collingwood, they had boarded the vessel for a Georgian Bay tour.

The *Ploughboy* encountered trouble near Lonely Island when the crosshead of her engine broke. The anchor was weighed and everyone aboard watched the horizon for signs of another vessel. When none arrived and the waves became choppy, the anchors began to drag. Slowly the steamer drifted towards the rocky coast of a nearby island. Other action had to be taken.

Some crew members were dispatched in a small boat for Owen Sound, a distance of seventy-five miles! Those remaining on board spent the next hours hoping and praying for some sort of salvation from their dilemma. Finally, in the early hours of the morning, the anchors once again caught hold and the vessel stopped its meandering drift to destruction. They lay only a mere 150 feet from certain peril. For the moment, at least, it seemed that they had been spared!

Meanwhile, the crew members who had gone for help, arrived in Owen Sound. Upon telling of the plight of their vessel, the steamer *Canadian* immediately pulled anchor and headed to the rescue. They found the *Ploughboy*, and took her in tow to Collingwood. Many of the *Ploughboy's* passengers took the first available train back to Toronto.[14]

On this 1877 visit, Macdonald travelled to Owen Sound by train, perhaps not wishing to risk fate again in the nearby waters of Georgian Bay! A royal welcome was planned for the arrival of Sir John and his entourage. The main thoroughfare, and many other streets in the community, were festooned with brightly coloured flags and banners well in advance of the momentous occasion. A welcoming party, speakers to pay tribute to Sir John, and other celebratory plans were put into place. However, something happened that the organizers had not counted upon. The train arrived ahead of schedule and it rained all day! Planned outdoor activities had to be shifted indoors and citizens crammed into the Queens Hotel to hear the grand old orator.

Sir John had not been the first distinguished visitor to Owen Sound in the 1870s. Three years earlier, on July 30, 1874, the Governor General, Lord Dufferin, [Frederick Temple Blackwood] arrived aboard the *Chicora.* As vice-regal tours were somewhat of a rarity in the Canadian hinterlands, Owen Sound's mayor, George Snider, was determined that this visit would not just go smoothly, but that it would be a memorable occasion!

Hence, it was decided that the main attraction of the visit was to be a stop at Inglis Falls. Many citizens, however, wondered at the folly of such an idea. During mid summer the falls was but a mere trickle of water!

A more recent look at Inglis Falls. *Photograph by Telfer Wegg.*

Five thousand area residents lined the harbour and the town's streets, eager to catch a glimpse of Lord and Lady Dufferin. The entourage made its way along the main thoroughfare and headed up the hill by the cemetery. At this point, a rider broke away from the entourage and sped ahead.

As the carriages turned in to the entrance leading to the falls, a sound could be heard that was usually only associated with springtime: the roar of torrents of water hurtling over the falls! Once all had witnessed the site of water thundering over the falls, the mayor seemed anxious to move on to the next stop on Dufferin's agenda. As they left, the last of the procession may have heard the noise of the rushing water diminishing. And that it was!

The mayor and the organizers had created a magnificent hoax to entertain the Governor General. During the spring of that year, volunteers, who had been sworn to secrecy, built a log dam a short distance up stream from the falls. Over the course of a few months the dam had held back the water. On the day of the vice-regal visit, the rider who had broken from the entourage at the cemetery hill had raced to the dam where a crew released some strategically placed logs. The freed water had rushed downstream and over the falls just as Lord Dufferin arrived upon the scene! Once again the ingenuity and determination of Owen Sounders had made the day![15]

19

ENTREPRENEURIAL GOODWILL
AND OPPORTUNITY

With the decade of the 1870s a new era of institutional and entrepreneurial energy came to Owen Sound. Correspondingly, the need for improved high school facilities became a popular topic in the community. Ultimately talk led to action and in 1878–79, land was purchased and a three-storey building was erected on land between 9th and 10th Streets 5th Avenue East. The cost of the land and the building was about $22,000.

In the 1850s, the colonial government of Upper Canada had legislated the creation of grammar schools. Then, the grammar schools were the first "secondary" schools and primary schools were known as common schools. In 1856, Grey County recognized a need to have a formal grammar school in the area. While a new building to house both the grammar and the common schools was being constructed on 10th Street West, about ten students were taught in a leased building on 3rd Avenue East. Unfortunately, problems arose with the new facility and the new school closed at the end of 1856. However, the need for a grammar school only intensified and, two years later, a new school was erected on 4th Avenue East, on the present site of Strathcona School.[1]

In 1886, the new high school was re-named the Owen Sound Collegiate and Vocational Institute (OSCVI). The dedication to academic excellence at the school was quickly illustrated when, from 1887–1892, the school placed first in the provincial departmental examinations.[2] In May 1952, the original school was destroyed by fire.

Owen Sound Collegiate and Vocational Institute in 1910. *Courtesy County of Grey-Owen Sound Museum.*

A new structure was opened in four years later, a further addition was completed in 1970, and in 1997, began construction on a new OSCVI at a new site on 8th Street East which was opened in the autumn of 1999.

Thousands of men and women have graduated from the OSCVI. Their contributions to society have not been limited to just this region. Many have gone on to gain recognition throughout the world. One of the more famous students to have attended this school is Agnes Campbell Macphail.[3] Born in Proton Township in the southern tier of Grey County, she attended the OSCVI for two years before enrolling in Normal School in Stratford. Agnes had an interest in politics and, it is said that on one occasion in 1919, she was called upon to speak at a political rally. At first she was reticent about speaking but before long tlhe audience seemed to cheer her every word. When she concluded, Agnes was hooked on politics. On December 6, 1920 Agnes Macphail made Canadian history when she was elected as the first female member of the House of Commons in Ottawa. For the next fourteen years she was the only woman in Parliament.

Another OSCVI student would gain international attention. Norman Bethune attended the OSCVI before moving to Gravenhurst, Ontario with his family. After becoming a doctor, Bethune gave up the traditional practice of medicine to travel to Spain and take part in the revolutionary wars which rocked that country in the 1930s. Dr. Bethune gained worldwide attention when he went to China and joined Mao Tse Tung's revolutionary forces. The graduate from the OSCVI is a revered figure in the history of China.

Throughout the history of Owen Sound, the ingenuity and determination of its citizens led to the creation of a very active Georgian Bay port. As already noted, the 1870s marked the beginning of a period of energetic expansion, sparked by the emergence of two dynamic entrepreneurs, S. Johnstone Parker and Richard Notter. Together, the two men were the driving force behind two utilities designed to greatly enhance life in Owen Sound.

Upon arrival in Owen Sound in 1865, Richard Notter established a general merchandise business and embarked on an active political career. Elected as a town

Richard Notter, a civic-minded dry goods merchant was mayor of Owen Sound in the late 1870s. His premature death was a loss to the community. Richard Notter is buried in Greenwood Cemetery. *Courtesy County of Grey-Owen Sound Museum.*

councillor on successive occasions, he also served two years as mayor in 1877–78,[4] as well as a director of the Toronto, Grey & Bruce Railway.

Shortly after Alexander Graham Bell's invention of the telephone in Brantford, Notter and Parker began their own telephone company in Owen Sound. The company was located in a back room of the second floor of a building at 878 2nd Avenue East, next door to Parker's drug store.

Due to the primitive nature of the operation, telephone service could not be extended to private homes. Instead, wires were strung to about twenty businesses located in the commercial section, the telephone system itself being powered by batteries located in each subscriber's location.

In 1884, a telephone system serving the broader community began. In that year, the Owen Sound Telephone Company Limited was formed with James McLauchlan as President and S.J. Parker as Vice-president. The company's headquarters remained on the second floor

S.J. Parker, a founding member of the Hospital Board, was a creative entrepreneur. Much of his energy was directed to the development of projects that would benefit the people of Owen Sound. *Courtesy County of Grey-Owen Sound Museum.*

of the Parker Block with lines strung througho the town.[5] While their original telephone proje was limited in scope, Parker and Notter's ne project would have a dramatic impact upon t entire community as the two men set out improve the town's water supply.

For some time, the quality of the town water F been a major concern to its citizens. Many peoj used barrels to collect rain water, then strained t water through a cloth to remove the impuriti hardly a satisfactory method to protect the co munity from disease. But obtaining fresh wa was not easy as the only other main source water was a spring near Inglis Falls, two to th miles to the south of the centre of the town.

Once Parker and Notter discovered that Ontario statute allowed the establishment of p vately operated waterworks systems, th researched the feasibility of establishing a wa works, negotiated an agreement with town cor cil and began construction. In order to facilit the project, the town council passed a bylaw 1879, allowing the two men to erect and hold the franchise for a wat works system. The cost to Notter and Parker was $35,000 and t town maintained the right to purchase the system, at an arbitrated f market value, within ten years. This was a multi-faceted project. N only did it meet the domestic needs of the community for clean wat it also provided for adequate water for fire emergencies.

The utility drew its water from a spring on the Creamery Hill, j two miles from the market square. The fact that the source was 1 feet above the city simplified distribution downstream. A water tov was built on the north side of 8th Street East[6] with two reservoirs the south side of the same street. Chlorination and filtration syste were installed to improve the water's drinking quality.[7] By the 188 the system was up and running and the town proclaimed a civic h day to honour the momentous occasion.

The technology involved to create the water works utility is anot example of the ingenuity of the entrepreneurs. A penstock, six feet eight feet and seven feet deep, was built at the source. Seven thous

The 1883 Owen Sound Board of Trade. Standing at back (l-r): Charles Conklin, ___ Coates, Wm. Masson, W.B. Stephens, R.P. Butchart. Seated (l-r): J.R. Brown, George Kilburn Sr., George I. Inglis, Wm. Brown (seated on high stool), Joseph Maughan. Seated on the floor: man left unidentified, on the right, John C. Crane. *Courtesy County of Grey-Owen Sound Museum.*

feet of piping, six inches in diameter and made from spruce logs, were laid from the penstock along the road atop the west hill to 8th Street West. At the top of this street the water flowed through iron pipes down to the market square and on to the reservoirs. At this point, it seems, pipelines branched throughout the community. The system had shut-off valves located at most intersections to assure adequate pressure in case of a fire emergency.

The cost to the consumer was $6.00 per year for a five-room house, with an extra charge of $1.00 if the house had a bath or a basin. An additional fee of $3.00 was levied if the house contained a water closet. There was also a surcharge for families whose number exceeded five. The community was charged fifty dollars for each of the twenty fire hydrants that were installed, while stores were charged an annual fee of $10.00.[8] A decade later the town exercised its option to purchase the utility.

Unfortunately, Notter died in 1883, at the young age of 43 years. Consequently, Parker had to find other partners when he undertook his next utility project, the Owen Sound Electrical Illumination and Manufacturing Company. Parker was the President of the company and his associates were William Brown, Edward Todd, and J.W. Redfern. In 1887, a small power plant was erected about a mile and a half above Inglis Falls,[9] to provide the power for the arc street lights in the community. Later, the company built a steam power plant on 1st Avenue East, just north of 10th Street.[10]

As with the water utility project, the community held an option to purchase the power company. This was exercised in 1903, when Owen Sound paid $36,000 for the company. By 1915, because of a rising demand for electricity, the city completed negotiations for power with the newly formed Ontario Hydro Commission. This enabled the community to draw its power from the generating installation located at Eugenia in Grey County.[11]

The development of Owen Sound had depended upon the entrepreneurial drive and the determination of the town's business community. In 1880, perhaps to help co-ordinate future efforts to further develop the town's prospects, the Board of Trade was incorporated. Originally this organization had been established in 1864, with David Christie as its first president.[11] At the forefront of this organization was its current president, the co-founder of Owen Sound's public utility operations, S.J. Parker.[13]

Anyone strolling along the main shopping street of Owen Sound would be attracted to the commercial establishments. Store windows have always been a means of advertising the goods and services offered by business establishments. However, more than a century ago an innovative Owen Sound entrepreneur tried something different.

Perhaps pedestrians thought it was an April Fools joke, after all it was April 1! The year was 1895 and it wasn't a prank. It was a unique attempt to bring attention to a new business on Owen Sound's main street.

David Creighton Taylor and his partner Ed Grier had opened a jewellery store. Taylor, a watchmaker, set up his work station in the window of his new store. A century ago mass-produced watches were virtually an unheard of commodity and watches were not sent off to the big city to be repaired. Instead, local artisans plied their trade on an individual basis in their store. Taylor took this one step further. By working in his store window, in full view of passersby, the whole world, at least Owen Sound's part of the world, could view the intricacies of watchmaking and repairs.

Family enterprises have always been a large part of Owen Sound's economic history. Names like Harrison, Kennedy and Stephens dot the landscape of this community's growth and development. David Creighton Taylor was a part of this tradition. His father Henry owned a tailor shop which was one of Owen Sound's first commercial estab-

The Owen Sound Clippers - the 1894 Northwestern Ontario Baseball Champions: back row (l-r): A.J. Creighton (Vice-President), M. Griffin (Manager), David Taylor (Captain), C. Dowding; middle row (l-r): P. Bailey, F.R. Glassford (Secretary-Treasurer), G.P. Taylor (President), G.D. McLaughlan, A. Brock; front row (l-r): W. Irving, C. Thompson, D. Christie.

lishments. His maternal uncle, David Creighton, was editor of the Owen Sound *Times*.

David decided to continue the family tradition of being involved in commercial enterprise, but chose to branch out into a new field, watchmaking. After two years of partnership with Grier, Taylor struck out on his own. In 1910 he formed a new partnership with J.J. Douglas, the man with whom he had apprenticed. This enterprise remained until 1928 when both men decided to part company, once each had a son ready to enter business.

Unfortunately, seventeen years after bringing his son Creighton into the business, tragedy struck. The younger Taylor was lost in a boating accident on Owen Sound bay in late October 1945. For the next six years, David Taylor would manage the business alone until his grandson and namesake David could continue in the tradition of his father and grandfather.

D.C. Taylor was also deeply involved in the life of his home town. A lover of music, he opened his store after hours for friends who of like appreciation. Out of these lively jam sessions, a group known as the "Bon Tons" was formed. Wearing striped suits and straw hats, the "Bon Tons" were a popular attraction at social engagements in the area. As well, Taylor was a supporter of baseball. Many early documents about the Owen Sound Clippers baseball team bear his name and picture.

Today the Taylor family is still involved in the business started by their great-grandfather more than a century ago. However, the tradition of making and repairing watches in the window of the store has faded with time.

Not unlike most communities in the nineteenth century, Owen Sound was vulnerable to the outbreak of epidemics of illnesses such as diphtheria, smallpox, scarlatina and many other maladies. Although the new water supply had reduced the frequency of these plagues, other factors made early residents susceptible to the rampant spread of such diseases.

Owen Sound municipal authorities seemed to ignore public health issues. Perhaps they did not possess adequate knowledge about the adverse impact of existing conditions on community health. Sanitation proceedures in butcher shops and dairies were not monitored. Consequently, customers "suffered the consequences, including death, of eating contaminated meat and drinking impure milk."[14] The slaughterhouses on the west side of the town "sluiced their offal directly into the bay."[15]

Private homes often ran their drainage directly into gutters along nearby road frontages. Because officials refused to enforce the bylaw restricting farm animals within the town limits, cattle and hogs roamed at will. Historian David Gagan reported that in 1890 there were 900 cattle and 232 hogs within the town limits. Perhaps this was one of the reasons that the death rate in Owen Sound in 1890 was twice the rate of rural Grey County. This circumstance combined with the number of horses required for transportation provided another severe problem concerning the uncontrolled presence of noxious wastes.[16]

Owen Sound's role as an important transportation centre also presented another source of disease. Hundreds, perhaps thousands, of people travelled through the port each year. These visitors had the use of one public well located near the CPR station. The risk of contamination was real. In 1888, the well had to be closed when it was learned that the clothing of a typhoid victim had been washed in the well.[17]

Through either incompetence or ignorance, or both, the commu-

A postcard view (c. 1907) of the Owen Sound General and Marine Hospital. The building was erected in 1893. *Courtesy County of Grey-Owen Sound Museum.*

nity continued to suffer from almost annual outbreaks of epidemics. Finally, in 1927, the city's water supply was discovered to be the main culprit. Steps were taken. In that year Owen Sound started chemically treating its water supply.[18]

The usual treatment for these diseases was the isolation of those who had become ill. The victims were either quarantined at home or, if available, in hospital. However, during this era, the hospitals that did exist were little more than isolation wards, offering minimal treatment, and always inadequate space. In fact, in an 1885 typhoid epidemic, a vacant house had to be rented to serve as a hospital. During the next few years, other outbreaks occurred. In 1889, a beleaguered medical community, proposed a more permanent solution to the care and treatment of patients.[19]

The area medical committee[20] felt

Dr. Allan Cameron, Owen Sound's Medical Officer of Health, and an unidentified nurse, with other nurses from the General and Marine Hospital in the background, 1903. Dr. Cameron had served the needs of the area for many years. *Courtesy County of Grey-Owen Sound Museum.*

that a permanent, multi-faceted hospital was necessary. By February 1889, they had a plan in place and had received a promise of a $1,000 grant from Grey County.[21] A presentation made to the town council resulted in more success for the project:

> "After a special committee had considered that matter for two weeks, the Owen Sound Town Council pledged $600 from its revenues, another $1,000 from a bequest left in trust to the town for charitable purposes, and a parcel of land in the south end of the town."[22]

This action drew the attention of the business community. Once again, civic-minded business leaders recognized that a hospital would not only solve a major problem, but that it would enhance Owen Sound's future. At the head of the list off businessmen spearheading the drive for a hospital was none other than S.J. Parker. Other prominent members of the commercial community involved were: Frederick d'Orr, a hardware merchant; William Roy, financier; John Harrison, sawmill operator; and J.M. Kilbourn, financier and barrister.

As a result of these efforts, the Owen Sound General and Marine Hospital officially opened on June 21, 1893. In 1918 the hospital purchased its first x-ray machine, however, the first x-ray technician was not an employee of the hospital. John James, a local photographer, in 1917 had provided both the x-ray machine and his services to the hospital. In 1918 the hospital acquired his equipment, but James continued to perform x-ray services until 1922 when Dr. E.E. Evans took over the duties and the hospital bought more powerful equipment.[23]

During the First World War the facilities and staff of the Owen Sound General Marine were faced with many difficult situations. In 1916, the 147th and 248th battalions of the Canadian Armed Forces trained in Grey County, and the Canadian Army Medical Corps used the hospital. Moreover, the facilities and civilian staff at the hospital still had to deal with the prescence of a large number of war-related casualties. However, these circumstances as well as the almost annual epidemic of typhoid in the region were minor in comparison to the malady which struck the area in 1918.

A world-wide epidemic of Spanish Influenza wreaked havoc on the local populace:

"The virus was introduced into the trenches of Europe by Chinese labourers employed by the British army. It spread quickly among the troops at the front and was soon transmitted to army camps in England and was then transported to North America by returning soldiers. The virus and its carriers fanned out across the country along the major transportation arteries until, by October 1918, Canadians everywhere had fallen victims to the world-wide pandemic of a particularly virulent strain of influenza characterized by abnormally high mortality rates, especially among 20–40 year olds."[24]

The Spanish Flu had a direct impact on the Owen Sound area. By October 1918 there were 800 reported cases and the Board of Health had closed all public meeting places such as schools, churches and theatres. The hospital facilities were over-taxed and teachers were recruited as volunteer nurses to care for those who could not be accommodated in the hospital. This epidemic lasted about forty-five days and the results were catastrophic. In all, there had been 2,000 reported cases in Owen Sound and twenty-one deaths, most of whom were young adults.[25]

20

RIVALRIES

The arrival of the railway in Owen Sound coincided with increased shipping activity throughout the Great Lakes region. The Georgian Bay ports, and indeed the entire Great Lakes system, vied for the attention of the growing upper lakes fleet. However, rivalries with two nearby ports, Wiarton and Collingwood, provided the most serious threats to Owen Sound's ambitions.

Although Wiarton initially had been settled almost a quarter of a century after the first settlers arrived in Owen Sound, the Colpoys Bay community through its newspaper, the *Echo*, provided vitriolic attacks against Owen Sound. The editor of the Wiarton paper spared nothing in his commentary in his efforts to influence a shift in maritime commerce from Owen Sound to his home town. An example of these attacks occurred in the October 31, 1879 edition:

"We are always reminded by our Owen Sound friends that their harbour is a model one; the finest, in fact, on the continent, and that ours is a "medium harbour." We are sorry we cannot ECHO their opinion. Experience will not warrant it: Last week the Frances Smith, heavily laden, called in there on her up trip, and was obliged to land her passengers at Boyd's old wharf, a mile and half out of town, for fear of sticking in the mud if she went into the harbour. The wharf was in shocking condition and ladies who were obliged to land did so at considerable risk, and were

104

compelled to walk a long distance over stones and other imped-
iments before they could reach the bus to take them into the
town. A truly magnificent harbour indeed, wharf and all, and we
think the least they say in its favour, and decry other and better
harbours the more it will become them."[1]

When it was learned that Owen Sound had petitioned the government to dredge its harbour, the *Echo* responded in its February 13,
1880 edition with: "Owen Sound has sent a deputation to Ottawa on
a begging expedition for their harbour." [2]

Owen Sound also competed with the port of Collingwood. The
political and commercial leaders of Owen Sound had long memories.
They remembered all too well Collingwood's victory in becoming the
northern terminus of the railway in the early 1850s. Consequently, the
ensuing two decades without a railway had created a determination in
Owen Sound that its interests would never want for effort!

One port facility that would help attract shipping traffic was a dry
dock. Here repairs could be made quickly and efficiently while the vessels unloaded and loaded their cargo. In February 1872, a campaign to
build a dry dock facility in Owen Sound had begun. At that time the
closest similar facility was located in Detroit. Those behind the building of a dry dock were convinced that expanding maritime activity on
the upper Great Lakes meant such an operation would be a boon to
Owen Sound's economy. Despite offers of lucrative grants from the
community, however, no one came forth immediately to take on the
project. Finally in September 1875, a group of community businessmen
formed the Owen Sound Dry Dock and Shipbuilding Company. With
the assistance of a $15,000 municipal grant, a dry dock 304 feet long,
75 feet wide and 16 feet deep was completed in June of 1877. Of note,
it was the only Canadian dry dock west of the Welland Canal.[3]

In April 1882, it was learned that Collingwood was considering
building a dry dock. Owen Sound interests saw this as a threat not
only to their dry dock, but also to their port function in general. The
Owen Sound *Advertiser* editorialized that there was a strong desire by
a few "citizens of Collingwood to do something to immortalize themselves" but that the voters "were not so blind as to throw away $25,000
merely to gratify the whims of a few interested parties."[4]

Later that month, the *Advertiser* hammered once again on the
theme of Collingwood's proposed new dry dock. This time the appear-

ance of Owen Sound's harbour and the folly of trying to compete with such a successful operation was the message conveyed:

"Last Monday our harbour presented an appearance which would have brought tears to the eyes of the strongest voter in Colling-wood. Both sides of the river were literally lined with magnificent steamboats and sailing vessels, actively engaged in receiving or dis-charging freight, painting, rigging and otherwise fitting out."[5]

After a decade of development due to the arrival of the railway to Owen Sound, the 1880s was marked by a period of continued attempts to increase the commercial activity in the harbour and therefore the entire business sector. The June 1, 1882 edition of the *Advertiser* reported that political and commercial leaders were joining forces with the Toronto, Grey & Bruce Railway in a plan to further increase rail and maritime traffic to Owen Sound. They planned to travel to Montreal to petition the Richelieu Steamship Company for service connecting Owen Sound and Lake Superior. Passengers and freight would then connect with lower Great Lakes destinations and on to Montreal where overseas travel could be facilitated with the Allan Steamship Line, thus creating commercial links between Lake Superior via Owen Sound to Liverpool, England.[6]

In the same month it was reported that the TG&B Railway was making plans for the construction of a grain elevator in Owen Sound. To ensure that the elevator was used to its capacity the company was negotiating with a steamship company to connect the port with Chicago and Duluth.[7]

In conjunction with this plan the *Advertiser* announced in the

Part of a Toronto Grey & Bruce Railway timetable, believed to be for the 1882 season. *Courtesy Grey County Archives.*

same issue that the *Africa* of the Northwestern Line of vessesls had arrived in Owen Sound. It is clear that both the newspaper and the TG&B Railway hoped that the arrival of the Northwestern vessel would divert traffic from Collingwood. The *Advertiser* reported: "We hope to see the line a success, and not let Collingwood have the trade which by rights belongs to Owen Sound."[8]

At the same time it was learned that another company had possible designs on operating out of Owen Sound. The July 6, 1882 edition of the *Advertiser* reported that the Canadian Pacific Syndicate had intentions to make Owen Sound the "headquarters from which to draw supplies for the construction of their road."[9] The editor wrote that the chief engineer, Mr. Abbott, was "strongly in favour of this port [Owen Sound], because it is by all odds the best place to collect supplies of grain and provisions, as well as materials wanted in the building of the road....[He] likes it better because he can save six hours on the trip from Algoma Mills to Toronto, and vice versa."[10]

A week later the *Advertiser* wrote an editorial of more far-reaching plans involving the CPR and Owen Sound. It was reported that the Toronto *World* had printed a story the previous day that as soon as the Thunder Bay section of the CPR rail line was completed, a line of steamers from either Lake Huron or Georgian Bay would be a more efficient link to the Canadian West than any other possible connections.[11] The *Advertiser* supported this claim with information that the *Campana* travelled from Owen Sound and Collingwood to Thunder Bay in forty hours. To increase the speed and perhaps reduce the cost, it was also suggested by the editor that the Toronto Grey & Bruce should be purchased by either the Grand Trunk or the CPR Syndicate. The argument continued in Owen Sound's favour from the prospective that a vessel sailing from Collingwood would take twelve hours longer because it would have to stop at both Meaford and Owen Sound. It was estimated that a trip from Owen Sound to the Lakehead would require twenty-four hours and an additional sixteen hours would land passengers and freight in Winnipeg forty hours after leaving Toronto.[12]

About the same time it was learned that the CPR might consider Owen Sound as the eastern terminus for its Great Lakes fleet. Not wanting a repeat of the 1852 situation when Owen Sound's lack of action had led to Collingwood's success in being named the northern terminus for the railroad, the business community of Owen Sound started immediate action. The *Advertiser* launched a media campaign

Yard of the Canadian Pacific Railway at Owen Sound, looking north, taken about 1900. The No. 1 and No. 2 sheds are to the left, with A and B elevators in the background. At right is the CPR Steamship office and next to it the Station. *Courtesy Grey County Archives.*

to promote Owen Sound. Journalists representing Toronto newspapers were invited to visit Owen Sound. Once they arrived they were the guests of honour at dinners and were given tours of the area pointing out the town's best features.

At the same time, a group of Owen Sound citizens formed a committee to consider ways of ensuring that the CPR selected this community as the eastern terminus for its Great Lakes fleet. A major factor in the CPR's decision would be the depth and access to the harbour. Therefore, they concluded that the harbour needed to be dredged. To ensure that the depth of the harbour could be continually maintained, it was decided that dredging equipment should be purchased. It was learned that the needed implements were about to go on sale at a nearby location, Collingwood!

The committee decided that James McLauchlan, owner of McLauchlan's Confectionary, would travel to Collingwood and, as discreetly as possible, purchase the necessary equipment. The group feared that if someone from Collingwood discovered that the dredging equipment was being purchased for use in Owen Sound's harbour, all efforts would be made to ensure that the machinery stayed in Collingwood!

To avoid detection, McLauchlan left for Collingwood by train from Meaford. Before the train entered Collingwood, he jumped from the car and unobtrusively made his way on foot to the sale. He successfully purchased one dredge, a tugboat and two scows. As he was about to leave town, McLauchlan realized that the remaining dredging equipment could still be purchased by Collingwood interests to bet-

The *Alberta*, one of the three vessels to sail from Owen Sound once the CPR made that port its eastern terminus. *Courtesy Grey County Archives.*

ter their harbour. He borrowed the necessary funds to make a ten per-cent down payment on the remaining dredge and two scows.[13]

When the ice disappeared from Owen Sound's harbour, the dredging operations began. These dredging efforts, combined with the previous operations carried out via allotments from the federal government had a significant impact upon the maritime access to Owen Sound harbour. "By 1884, Owen Sound's harbour boasted a channel 2,400′ long, 60′ wide and 16′5″ deep, and was not surpassed on the upper lakes for ease of access."[14]

A short time later the CPR announced that Owen Sound had been selected as the eastern terminus for its Great Lakes fleet, much to everyone's delight. The clandestine efforts and the investments of the committee had been successful. Revenge had been achieved for the slight of Owen Sound in the railway decision of 1852.

OWEN SOUND AND THE CPR

The CPR's impact on the economic growth of Owen Sound began almost at once. On July 26,1883, the company announced that its subsidiary, the Ontario and Quebec Railway, had leased the Toronto, Grey & Bruce Railway for 99 years at an annual rental of $140,000. The company began construction the following year on a 250,000 bushel grain elevator and purchased the wooden steamer, the *Georgian*:

> "Owen Sound felt the benefits of the CPR connection immediately, as over $4,000 a month in construction wages alone were injected into the community. A local mill supplied most of the one million feet of lumber used in building the elevator which was completed in August 1884, at a cost of $92,000. An additional $8,800 was spent erecting the CPR's freight, coal and immigrant sheds, passenger station and laundry. By year's end, an estimated $235,000 had been spent on new dwellings and businesses..."[1]

Excitement further increased in May 1884 when the *Algoma, Alberta,* and the *Athabaska* arrived in port after a unique voyage. The $300,000 vessels had been built in Scotland and sailed across the Atlantic. At 270 feet in length, they were too long to pass through the St. Lawrence canal system. Necessity prevailed and the three vessels were cut in half, sent through the canal and towed to Buffalo for reassembly. The upper

A fleet of Chicago grain vessels at Owen Sound near the CPR's Elevator A, built in 1885. In 1897, a second elevator was built near Elevator "A". Both were destroyed by fire in December, 1911. *Courtesy County of Grey-Owen Sound Museum.*

Great Lakes had probably never been traversed by such state of the ships! They could each accommodate 130 first class passengers with steerage bunks for 200 more. Their freight capacity was 2,000 tons. Electric lights were powered by on board generaters and they each had two steel masts and canvas for use in the event of engine trouble.[2]

Their value to the CPR and to the economy of Owen Sound was proven in the first season that they sailed between Owen Sound and Port Arthur. During the autumn of 1884 shipments of grain from Owen Sound to Montreal averaged 20,000 bushels a day as the *Algoma* and the *Athabaska* completed a record-breaking twenty-eight round trips between Owen Sound and the lakehead of Superior.[3]

The benefit to Owen Sound did not cease with the close of the navigation season. During the winter of 1884, twelve steamers, eight schooners, six tugs and one barge wintered in the harbour.[4]

Despite all the preparation, within three years of the inauguration of CPR operations in Owen Sound it was evident that the existing facilities were inadequate. With the CPR vessels receiving priority in unloading and loading at the elevator, other vessels had to endure costly delays. Consequently, many non-CPR vessels started to by-pass Owen Sound in favour of other ports. Fewer ships entering the port meant less work and income for independent businesses and labourers.

In the spring of 1890, a fleet of CPR steamships are docked in Owen Sound, (from l-r) the *Athabaska*, the *Alberta* and the *Manitoba*. At the extreme right the steamer, the *City of Midland*, is under construction for the North Shore Navigation Company. *Courtesy Grey County Archives.*

Over almost the entire next decade the town and the CPR were at loggerheads over the construction of another larger elevator. In 1897, the CPR issued a threat which the town could not ignore. Two years earlier the company had "...offered to build a 1,050,000 bushel elevator, and increase its flour shed capacity from 6,000 to 30,000 barrels."[5] The company wanted a $40,000 bonus from the town and an assessment totalling $100,000 for all of its present and future properties in Owen Sound for a period of twenty-one years. The CPR also promised to replace the elevators if either of them were destroyed within the next thirty years or repay the town the outstanding balance of the $40,000 debenture.[6] In 1897, the General Superintendent of the CPR, J.W. Leonard, arrived in Owen Sound and urged the electorate to pass the necessary bylaw which would allow the company's 1895 offer to be fulfilled.

Leonard suggested that if the town did not agree to their proposal then the company might have to take its business to another Georgian Bay port. The Owen Sound *Times* responded to this threat by reminding its readers of the error made in the early 1850s when the community failed to offer a bonus incentive to railway builders and Owen Sound was ignored in favour of Collingwood. The electorate responded and on February 15, 1897, they supported the CPR plan by a vote of 257 to 140.[7]

The issuing of the bonus to the CPR had payoffs for the town from its onset. In 1897, "the CPR spent an estimated $250,000 in Owen

This view of the *Aurora* (at the left) with the Canadian Pacific Railway grain elevator on the east side of Owen Sound Harbour, was used on a promotional poster by the CPR. *Courtesy County of Grey-Owen Sound Museum.*

Sound," including "more than $40,000" in wages. As well as the new elevator, the harbour now had more than "1200 feet of freight sheds, seven miles of railway sidings, and a harbour twenty feet deep." The value of CPR properties, in Owen Sound, including steamers, totalled approximately $3,000,000.[8]

However, the grain trade had not matched the expectations of Owen Sound's economic and political leaders. By late summer in 1900, only 58,000 bushels had been stored in the elevator and the new facility was virtually empty. Many criticized the town for extending a bonus to the CPR without a provision that the company must meet an annual minimum in terms of grain shipments.[9]

This circumstance led many civic leaders to call for the construction of another independent grain elevator to attract vessels outside of the CPR fleet. Status quo was not sufficient. Indeed, the 1890s marked an era of promotional attempts to further broaden Owen Sound's economic base.

Railway connections for the community continued to be a major issue for the leaders of Owen Sound's political and economic community, even after the TG&B Railway arrived in the 1870s. The sentiment seemed to be that if one railway was good, more than one rail connection would be better. In 1891, the opportunity to test this theory arose when the Grand Trunk Railway which served the port of Wiarton offered to build a spur line from Park Head, a small village on the border between Grey and Bruce counties, to Owen Sound through Brooke.[10]

Owen Sound granted the Grand Trunk Railway a $75,000 bonus and construction on the line began, with the first train arriving to a grand reception on July 12, 1894.[11] Not unexpectedly, the arrival of the GTR did not go unnoticed by the CPR, and the leaders of that company tried to discourage Owen Sound's decision to bring another rail line into the community.[12]

The first Grand Trunk train arrived in Owen Sound from Palmerston, amid great fanfare, at about 10:00 am on July 12 with nine coaches filled to capacity in honour of the occasion, accompanied by a band from Chesley. At noon another train chugged into the station pulling ten cars loaded with passengers from Stratford and points in between. This train carried two bands, one each from Listowel and Tara, to celebrate the momentus event. Soon after, yet another train of ten cars arrived from Guelph carrying a full contingent of passengers. At about the same time, the *Pacific* sailed into port from Collingwood and Meaford to join in the festivities. The *Times* reported that "altogether some 3,000 people" came to Owen Sound to join the large throngs of local citizens in the celebrations and that "the streets of the town have scarcely ever—if ever—been more densely crowded."[13]

The town had attempted unsuccessfully on many occasions to strike a deal with the Grand Trunk to build an elevator in the harbour. However, despite these failures, it is argued by many historians that the Owen Sound harbour was one of the busiest on the upper Great Lakes. Historian, Keith Fleming described the activity during the 1903 sailing season as follows:

"Each week during the 1903 navigational season the three CPR steamers sailed directly to Sault Ste. Marie and Fort William; four liners of the Northern Navigation Company and two from the Algoma Central Railway called at Owen Sound and all North Shore ports as far west as Sault Ste. Marie; the Dominion Fish Company's steamer completed the Soo-Mackinac run; and four other steamers maintained regular routes throughout Georgian Bay. Numerous unscheduled coal, lumber, grain and freight boats called at Owen Sound as well. Transshipments increased accordingly, with 346,949 tons of through freight, and 3,248,089 bushels of grain passing through the port in 1903."[14]

Locomotive #369 of the Grand Trunk Railway. The man on the left is David Muir, the other man is not identified. *Courtesy County of Grey-Owen Sound Museum.*

One of the major problems concerning maritime trade is that it is seasonal, and consequently, a large number of the workers did not work all year. In the late 1890s and the first decade of this century this circumstance led to labour unrest in Owen Sound. The workers of the area formed a loose collective to better their employment conditions.

On October 7, 1897 when the dock workers left their work at 6:00 pm they were told by the CPR to return in one hour, prepared to work all night. When the workers returned at seven o'clock, they demanded a raise of 2.5 cents, which would increase their hourly rate to fifteen cents. With two vessels waiting to be unloaded and another expected the next morning, the CPR was forced to agree to these terms. However, the next season, the company retaliated, by refusing to rehire the strikers.

In September 1899, with the harbour lined with ships waiting to be unloaded, the dock workers once again went on strike. They returned to work after four days of negotiations.

During this era there were frequent confrontations between the strikers and hired strike breakers. Perhaps the most volatile of the confrontations between the CPR and dock workers occurred in May 1908. When 170 workers walked off the job, the company responded by bringing in 100 workers by train from Toronto. These men were convinced by the strikers to join them rather than unload the ships. The next day the company brought in 200 more strike breakers. Like the first arrivals from Toronto, these men, too, were convinced to join the strike.

On Monday, May 11, an early morning train brought 70 additional workers to the docks. When the strikers learned that ships were being unloaded, they charged to the docks and became embroiled in a fierce battle with fifty CPR constables. Perhaps because of the overwhelming number of strikers and their supporters, the constables reacted by

115

Mayor Matthew Kennedy with Charles Gordon, Town Clerk, behind him to the right. In front is T.I. Thomson, owner of a hardware store in Owen Sound, an alderman at the time. Matthew Kennedy, son of William Kennedy was a successful politician and industrialist. *Courtesy County of Grey-Owen Sound Museum.*

firing shots into the mob.

Conditions remained tense until Mayor Matthew Kennedy read the Riot Act from the deck of a nearby steamer. Negotiations continued and at 1:30 pm the workers returned to their jobs with an agreement which paid them "15 cents an hour for day work, 16 cents an hour for night work, and 20 cents an hour for unloading coal and grain." The strike breakers all received free return passage by train to their homes in Toronto.[15]

Perhaps the strike had heightened labour awareness in the town as, in 1910, the Moulders Union gained recognition at the Empire Stove plant and shortly thereafter a Trades and Labour Council was formed in Owen Sound.[16]

Although there had been some difficulties between the town and the CPR, the benefits of being the eastern terminus of the CPR fleet far outweighed the detriments. Consequently, community leaders and citizens alike in Owen Sound were aghast upon hearing of a speech that CPR Vice-president David McNicoll delivered at the King Edward Hotel in Toronto on April 29, 1911. The speech revealed that the CPR intended to move its entire fleet operations from Owen Sound to Victoria Harbour, which was a short distance from its direct route between Toronto and Sudbury. If there was any question of the CPR's plans to leave Owen Sound, all doubts disappeared on the night of November 11, 1911, when a fire destroyed both grain elevators.[17] The irony of this night is that the downtown section of town was filled to capacity with a crowd celebrating the record majority victory by A.G. MacKay in that day's provincial

election. The mob of celebrants quickly dispersed to the docks and helped fight the fire and save two vessels, the *Keewatin* and the *Athabaska*, both of which were moored near the flaming elevators.

For the next fourteen years the grain trade by-passed Owen Sound. Finally, after struggling to find a company to build a new elevator complex in the harbour, the city decided to finance construction itself. In order to carry out the financing of the new elevator the city had to petition the provincial government to amend the statutes to enable a municipality "to build, lease, operate and sell terminal grain elevators."

The new elevator opened in November 1925, and its success was so immediate that the one million bushel elevator was soon inadequate to service the needs of the grain train entering the harbour.

T. I. Thomson was mayor in the late 1890s. Central to his political platform was the promotion of industrial and commerical development. *Courtesy County of Grey-Owen Sound Museum.*

The *Keewatin*, a CPR steamer, was one of the most luxurious cruise vessels of its era. Built to resemble an ocean-going vessel, the *Keewatin* cruised Georgian Bay providing regular passenger service for several decades following her inauguration circa 1910. *Courtesy County of Grey-Owen Sound Museum.*

A 1913 postcard view of Owen Sound Harbour, still showing the east side elevators that burned in 1911. *Courtesy County of Grey-Owen Sound Museum.*

Consequently, the elevator's capacity was doubled in 1927. However, this expansion project still failed to meet the needs of vessels using the harbour. As a result in 1929, four years after its construction, the elevator's capacity was once again increased. The elevators could now contain 4 million bushels![18]

Although many in the community were devastated by the loss of the CPR elevators and the railway's move to Port McNicoll others felt Owen Sound's economic base had developed to the point it could stand the shock. On February 2, 1912 the Owen Sound *Sun* issued a brave declaration, designed no doubt to raise civic spirits and put a positive spin on the recent events. The editor wrote, "...now is as good time as any to let it be known that Owen Sound is past the stage of swaddling clothes, that it can stand alone, and that whether the CPR goes or stays, Owen Sound will still be on the map."[19]

As the smoke of the last CPR steamer disappeared on the horizon leaving Owen Sound for the last time, it marked the end of an era. During its almost three decades as the eastern terminus of CPR Great Lakes fleet, Owen Sound had experienced dramatic growth. The following illustration by historian Keith Fleming shows the magnitude of this impact:

"In 1881, 327 persons, or 7.4% of its population [of] 4,426 were employed in Owen Sound's sixty-seven, primarily service-oriented manufacturing establishments. Averaging 4.9 employees per establishment, the town approached south-central Ontario's norm of 5.1. With a combined capital of $217,775, or $3,250 a piece, the aggregate production of Owen Sound's manufactories was $420,249. Finally, the town boasted some 173 commercial establishments with an aggregate fiscal strength of approximately $500,750.

"Over the ensuing thirty years, Owen Sound's population rose by 183.7% to 12,558, markedly higher than the provincial increase of 137%. The fifty-five manufacturing establishments employed 1,781 persons, or 14.2% of the population. This too was noteworthy since only five centres in south-central Ontario employed more than 2,000 workers in manufacturing. Owen Sound's average of 32.4 employees per industry also surpassed the provincial norm of 29.8. Of Grey County's workforce engaged in manufacturing in 1911, 45% were employed in Owen Sound, up from 14% in 1881. By 1911, the combined capital of the town's manufactories was $3,895,586, having risen 1,689% since 1881. The average capital of each manufacturer simultaneously increased twenty-one fold to $70,829, while their aggregate production rose 579% to $2,852,267. Dunn and Bradstreet, a financial services company, accounted for 315 commercial establishments with a combined fiscal strength estimated conservatively at $4,123,250, representing an increase of 723% over 1882."[20]

It is obvious the hard work and innovative ideas of the community's political and economic leaders had paid dividends. Despite the loss of the CPR fleet, Owen Sound's economic base was relatively secure.

22

BROADENING ECONOMIC HORIZONS

The designation of Owen Sound as the eastern terminus of the CPR Great Lakes fleet had provided yet another impetus to the economic growth of the town. On November 5, 1885, the CPR steamer, *Algoma*, sank on Lake Superior. The November 12, 1885 edition of the Owen Sound *Sun* reported the impact that this disaster had on the community (only 12 crew members and 2 passengers survived). The paper gave a partial list of the 39 who perished. They included Mrs. Dudgeon of Owen Sound and her two children, Mr. and Mrs. Edward L. Frost of Owen Sound, A. McKenzie, C. Taylor, James J. Scott, I. Bates, __ Ballantyne, F. Knight, T. McKeny, H. Emerson, H. McClinton, and Mrs. Shannon, __ Gill of Markdale and two Buchanan brothers.

To replace the *Algoma,* the CPR awarded a contract for $132,000 to the Polson Iron Works of Toronto to build a new vessel. The contract in itself was an innovative step for the Canadian shipbuilding industry. The new CPR vessel, *Manitoba*, would not only be the first steel steamer ever built in Canada,[1] but it would also be the largest steamer on the Great Lakes.

"The Manitoba had an overall length of 305 feet with a 38 foot beam. The hold depth was 14.3 feet. She had 146 frames (ribs) and seven bulkheads dividing her into eight watertight compartments and was classed as 100 A by the Lloyd's shipping registry.

Some 1,100 tons of steel was used in her construction giving her a measurement of 2,616 gross tons. Her upper deck was to be 250 feet long with 64 staterooms, all finished in antique oak." [2]

The *Manitoba*, would be an entirely new vessel except for the boilers and engine which had been salvaged from the *Algoma*.[3] Despite winning this contract, Polson's did not have access to a shipyard capable of this project. After approaching

The wreck of the *Algoma*, a CPR steamer, sunk off Isle Royal in Lake Superior in the fall of 1885. *Courtesy Grey County Archives.*

several communities, Polson's decided to build a shipyard in Owen Sound. Interestingly, various sources indicate that this was not the first shipbuilding venture in Owen Sound,[4] the first vessel having been built there in the late 1840s. It seemed logical that Poulson's should build the vessel close to the CPR fleet's home port. Owen Sound realizing the value of such an enterprise on their harbourfront, helped Polson's reach this decision by making an attractive offer to entice them to locate here. The company was offered "a free building site, freedom from taxation for ten years as well as the required dredging for the launching basin."[5]

The Polson complex included machine, woodworking, blacksmith and furnace shops, as well as 900 feet of water front on the east side of the harbour. The overall enterprise provided employment for 300 workers,[6] and quite a number of expert shipbuilders from the Clyde plants in Scotland were brought out to Owen Sound to work in the yards.[7] In later years this same location would be the site of Russell Brothers Shipbuilders.

Owen Sound's leaders soon realized that they had made a mistake in offering to build Polson's a launching basin. However, using the creativity for which they had come to be known, an alternative less costly plan was devised. They passed a bylaw which allowed the town to grant the company "$15,000 to purchase the Owen Sound Dry Dock and to undertake the remainder of the dredging"[8] that was necessary.

The *SS Manitoba*, ready to be launched at the Polson Shipyards, Owen Sound, on May 4, 1889. The picture was taken as the crowd was gathering for the event. The railway car on the tracks in the foreground, known as a "palace car," had brought a party of prominent railway and public officials to witness the event. *Courtesy Grey County Archives.*

When the CPR steamer, the *Manitoba* was built, she was considered the "last word" in ship construction on the Great Lakes, the largest and finest vessel on the Canadian side. *Courtesy Grey County Archives.*

The building of the *Manitoba* was fraught with costly complications, but finally, she was launched in May 1889. While the Polson yards continued to build steel vessels in Owen Sound, continued problems soon embedded the company deeply in financial disaster. The work of completing the vessel consumed the remainder of 1889. Business conditions

A photograph of the officers of the *Manitoba*, the popular CPR passenger steamer, taken about 1896. Front row (l-r): Jack Currie, Owen Sound, second mate; Wm. Bethune, Seaforth, purser; M. Cooney, Detroit, chief steward; Thos. Greig, Owen Sound, chief engineer; back row (l-r): Wm. Lewis, Owen Sound, chief engineer; Capt. Edward Anderson, Owen Sound; Thomas Martin, Owen Sound, first mate; Captain Anderson was in charge of the *Manitoba* from its first trip in 1889 until his retirement in 1908. He was a resident of Owen Sound for many years. *Courtesy Grey County Archives.*

were so bad that it was not until May, 1891 that the *Manitoba* left Owen Sound on its first trip to the head of the lakes.[9] In 1893, Polson's Shipyards closed their Owen Sound operations.[10]

This economic setback did not deter growth in Owen Sound. In 1897, the town published a promotional pamphlet with the rather lengthy title: *Some Views in and Around the Town of Owen Sound— The Capital of the County of Grey, in the Province of Ontario, with a Short Write-up of the Many Advantages to be Derived Through Living, and Doing Business There, Its Past, Present, and Bright Future.* Produced under the auspices of Mayor T. I. Thomson and the Board of

Poulett Street, the commercial district of Owen Sound, as it would have appeared in the 1890s, facing south from 10th street. Note the City Hall clock tower (with dummy clock) centre right at the top of the photograph. *Courtesy County of Grey-Owen Sound Museum.*

Trade, this publication illustrated the community's growth in the recent past and trumpeted the expected growth in the future.[11]

The 1909 *Port Directory* seems to bear out the predictions of the community leaders in 1897. That publication presents a picture of Owen Sound's harbour as a hive of activity. It lists 11 different wharves on the east side of the harbour and nine on the west side.[12] Despite the CPR moving its headquarters to *Port McNicoll* in 1912, the *Port Directory of 1923* illustrates that Owen Sound's maritime economic foundation, although slightly diminished, remained strong. Eleven wharves were still in operation on the east side. The only change in corporate ownership concerned the Northern Navigation Company wharf which was now owned by Dominion Transportation Company. The number of wharves on the west side had been reduced by one as the Grey and Bruce Cement Company was no longer listed in the Directory.

The 1909 *Directory* reported that the total tonnage entering the port in 1908, not including vessels which cleared the harbour, amounted to 479,906 tons. The 1923 report illustrates that the loss of the CPR had affected maritime traffic, but port facility was still quite active.[13]

Further statistics illustrate that Owen Sound's official designation as a city in 1920 did not come unwarranted. The value of Owen Sound's assets, $2,066,126, ranked them in fourteenth place in the province of Ontario. In fact, this community was within a million dollars of much larger centres such as Sault Ste. Marie, Peterborough, Kitchener, and Guelph. In an other important category, the value of municipalities per capita, Owen Sound ranked seventh[14] in the province.[15]

During the last quarter of the nineteenth century Owen Sound had benefitted from a change in entrepreneurial attitude in North America. At first, business ventures had tended to be the result of efforts by individuals or family members. However, as the North American economy became more diversified, increasing entrepreneurial opportunity created mergers and conglomerates between industrialists and businessmen.

In the 1890s, James McLauchlan, an Owen Sound confectioner, created McLauchlan Park a few miles to the north of the town on the west shore of the bay at the present day site of Balmy Beach. Also known as the Pleasure Grounds, this enterprise soon became a major attraction for local citizens wishing to while away the hours fishing, swimming, lawnbowling, or just lazing in the sun enjoying the balmy breezes off the bay.

At this time in North America, tourism was becoming an important industry as increased industrialization and new inventions allowed for more leisure time. Perhaps recognizing this trend and becoming aware of a boom in tourism in Ontario's Muskoka district, McLauchlan launched a plan to create a tourist facility in this area.

In 1901, McLauchlan created the Georgian Bay Summer Park and Resort Company, and he invited other area businessmen to join in this venture. As a result, the board of directors of the new company represents a virtual "who's who" of Owen Sound's commercial and industrial elite. Some of those who served on the board included David Martin Butchart, Fred W. Harrison, Mr. Hay, Judge A.D. Creasor, and Christopher Eaton.

The King's Royal Hotel as shown on an early souvenir postcard. *Courtesy Barry Penhale Collection.*

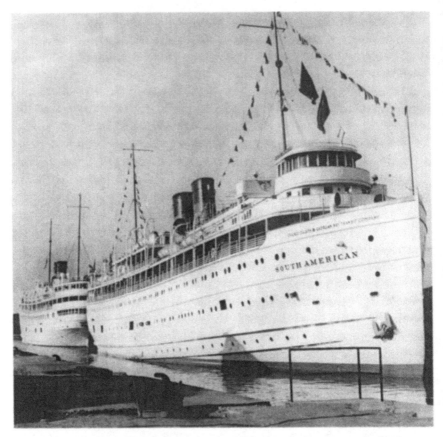

Cruise ships such as the *South American*, and the *North American* in the background, were regular visitors to Owen Sound. These luxury liners carried tourists to the King's Royal Park and to Georgian Bay ports for many decades. According to the memories of some early residents, when these ships called in Owen Sound some passengers would throw pennies into the water and local children would dive in to retrieve them. *Courtesy Grey County Archives.*

The company planned to build a complex known as King's Royal Park. In order to compete successfully with the popular Muskoka tourist meccas, King's Royal Park was designed to be opulent beyond the terms of its time. The red tile roof with white exterior, Spanish-style, 100-room hotel was erected in less than a year. The ornate, wrought-iron balconies were designed to give guests a spectacular view of Georgian Bay.

At the private dock arriving guests could enjoy the natural environment of the area, play golf, tennis, lawnbowl or simply relax indoors in the one of the many private sitting and writing rooms or in the billiard rooms. The evenings featured dancing in the ballroom and fine dining. The lavish structure also boasted its own theatre!

At first, King's Royal Park was a smashing success. Cruise vessels brought tourists from all over the mid-western United States and Canada. But gradually, interest in holidaying on the shores of Owen Sound decreased. By the beginning of the First World War registration at the hotel was less than 10 percent of capacity. In 1916, the majestic structure was sold to a Toronto wrecking company for a mere $5,200![16]

Today, King's Royal Park is but a memory. Where the once majestic hotel stood, now modern homes line the shoreline of Balmy Beach. But, if you look carefully into the water, when the light is just right you can see the pillars of old pier. On warm summer evenings, if you listen carefully and let your imagination wander you might hear the sounds of a band playing or the laughter of tourists enjoying the luxurious life of King's Royal Park.

In 1909, the map of Owen Sound experienced a dramatic change. On February 20, 1909, the community of Brookholm, or Brooke, as it was more popularly known was legally separated from Sarawak township and amalgamated with Owen Sound.

This merger of the two communities was the result of more than a decade of lobbying by citizens from both communities who felt that unification would benefit everyone. Afterall, both Owen Sound and Brooke had social and economic links. Consequently, their growth and development had marched along in step almost since the birth of Brooke in the 1850s.

However, not all of the original community of Brooke was amalagamated with Owen Sound. The area annexed to Owen Sound stretched from the harbour to the east side of 8th Avenue West and north a short distance beyond the present day location of the Yacht Club. The remaining part of Brooke, known as Rockview, a plot of land about two and one half square miles in size remained part of Sarawak township.

Brooke's emergence as a community had commenced almost immediately after the signing of the 1857 treaty with the Native People of the area which opened almost all of the "Indian" Peninsula for settlement. Lord Bury who served as Chief Superintendent of Indian Affairs at the time of the treaty signing, named Brooke after James Brooke who had acted as a Colonial overseer of Sarawak, a region of northwest Borneo. Bury, likewise, gave the township the name of Sarawak. The treaty also led to the creation of two new Grey County townships, Keppel and Sarawak. At first, they were united as one political entity until 1868 when they were given independence from each other. Brooke was forced to change its name to Brookholm because postal authorities preferred that name to avoid confusion because there was another Brooke located elsewhere in southern Ontario.[17]

Rose MacLeod in her history of the region, *Sarawak Saga*, described the conditions that early settlers of Brooke found when they arrived:

"The early settlers, on cutting the trees to build their houses and barns, were happily surprised to find that scarcely any stones marred the fertile clearings. Large gardens were soon producing fruit and vegetables for the townsfolk and small dairy herds were providing milk and cream."[18]

Brookholm's main street was Market Street (4th Avenue West), a main thoroughfare that ran from Griffith Hill (25th Street) south to the Pottawattomi River. There was no bridge between Brookholm's main street and the community of Owen Sound. Travellers had to follow the rather circuitous route up what is today 15th Street to Wright's mill dam and then down Mill Road (14th Street West).[19]

Today, the division between Owen Sound and Brooke is virtually invisible to all but those who remember the "old days" when the rivalry between the two communities was as intense as the competitive feelings between Owen Sound and its two neighbouring port communities of Wiarton and Collingwood.

23

THE CITY OF OWEN SOUND

The 1920s marked a new era in the history of Owen Sound. No longer was it a community striving to succeed as an outpost of civilization in a sparsely populated and relatively unknown section of Ontario. In 1920 it received its designation as a city, and it still had a reputation as an important Georgian Bay port. The face of the city had changed dramatically from its pioneer days. Stately homes lined the streets, the harbour was an entrenched centre of industrialism, but most of all the main commerical section resembled anything but a community on the verge of growth. Owen Sound had arrived.

"If one should stand on this street (2nd Avenue East) opposite the city hall, and look northward, he would observe in the next two blocks, the heart and business centre of the city. On either side, between eighth and tenth street, there are over a hundred business houses, representing no less than twenty-five different departments of business, besides numerous offices of professional men, companies, and local agencies."[1]

The industrial segment of Owen Sound's economic life was diversified and well-developed. The Wm. Kennedy and Sons and Harrison Mills enterprises were still going strong after more than a half century of operations. The North American Bent Chair Company had rebuilt after its disastrous fire in 1899. Keenan Brothers, established in 1896,

The North American Bent Chair Company rebuilt their operation after the fire of 1899. In 1920, the baseball team they sponsored captured the city baseball championship: back row (l-r): A.S. Miller, F.W. Harris, J.A. Minchner, Joe Ramsay, George Foote, Edward Irving, M. Tansley, R.S. Brown; middle row (l-r): J. Calcott, R. Flanigan, E. Tuckwell, R. Miller, W. Vance; front row (l-r): A. Levi, L. McDonald, Roy Taylor (Mascot), Fred Foote, E. Jarvis. *Courtesy County of Grey-Owen Sound Museum.*

had diversified their operations. In 1904, they broadened their scope with the purchase of the Parkhill Basket Company and, in 1917, they further increased their base of operations with the purchase of the Eureka Refrigerator Company. As well, Keenans operated the Keenan Towing Company with a fleet consisting of the tug, *Keenan* and two barges, the *McGill* and the *McWilliams*.[2]

More recently new industrial enterprises had begun operating in Owen Sound. The Owen Sound Cereal Mills replaced the former Duncan Haston Company in May, 1920. A few months later the Aluminum Steel Products company opened its doors. On the eastern shore of the harbour the Northern Bolt, Screw and Wire Company, established in the middle of the previous decade, continued to grow and prosper.

In 1921, a group of city entrepreneurs formed the Owen Sound Transportation Company. Their first vessel, a steamer the *Michipi-*

coten, sailed until it was replaced in 1927 by the *Manitoulin*. A year later, the company added the *Manasoo* to its fleet. In 1949, the *Manitoulin* was retired and the next sailing season saw the *Norgoma* working under OSTC colours between the ports of Owen Sound, Manitoulin Island and Sault Ste. Marie.

During this period, another pillar of the city's industrial sector, Richardson, Bond and Wright Limited began printing operations. Other industries active during this era included the North American Furniture Company, the Owen Sound Chair Company, the Owen Sound Wire Fence Company and the Empire Stove Company.

For many decades safety on the Great Lakes was a topic of much discussion. However, little if any action was taken to make sailing safer. Finally, in 1920, sailors in Owen Sound took matters into their own hands.

In January 1920, at a meeting in the Owen Sound City Hall, local sailors listened to a presentation by Captain Strain, a mariner from Buffalo, New York. Strain was the first vice-president of the Masters, Mates and Pilots Association. This organization not only represented its members in wage negotiations, it also held training seminars directed at safe working conditions for sailors. Strain pointed out to his audience that American vessels charged the same cargo rates as their Canadian counterparts, yet the American sailors received higher pay and showed a better record of sailing safety. At the end of the meeting, the Owen Sound sailors voted in favour of establishing the first Canadian chapter of the Masters, Mates and Pilots Association.

In 1920, it was also announced that George Brookes planned to operate an airline between Toronto and Owen Sound. Some citizens were concerned about the safety of such a venture, but the *Sun Times*, perhaps to allay these fears, quoted Mr. Brookes as saying "a person is quite as safe in an aeroplane as in an automobile, and a great deal safer than a pedestrian crossing 2nd Avenue East on a busy day in the summer time."[3]

Owen Sound celebrated its becoming a city on July 1, 1920 in grand fashion. The process by which Owen Sound became a city was surprisingly short, but not without some controversy. It had only been a few months earlier, on March 8, 1920, when civic leaders began their quest to achieve status as city. From that point, it had only taken a few months to earn the desired goal. But sailing towards city status was not without some rough times.

An Owen Sound Baseball Club of 1901: top inset (l-r) George Lacaille (Manager), B. Wanless (1st base), John Crate (press reporter); back row, standing (l-r) E. Fox, H. Ross, John H. McLaughlan (President), Dr. E.H. Horsey (MP Hon. President), Alderman Harrison, Jas. M. Brandon, W. Miller; middle row, sitting (l-r) A. McDonald (right field), Joe Ramsay (2nd base), R.M. Asher (centre field), H. Williams (pitcher), A. McPhatter (catcher); front row (l-r) T. Simms (3rd base), R. Christie, John B. Coates (left field). *Courtesy County of Grey-Owen Sound Museum.*

When the proposal was made on March 8, Mayor Roland Patterson read a report from the law firm of Wright, Birnie and Telford which stated that after studying the proposal, it was felt that if Owen Sound separated from Grey County and became a city it would result in a savings of $16,600 for Owen Sound taxpayers. One week after this meeting, Owen Sound Council met in a special session to enact a bylaw proposing application to the provincial legislature to become a city.

Owen Sound's actions brought a swift reponse from Grey County. At meetings held on March 25–26, County Council voted to oppose Owen Sound's application to the provincial government. Later on March 26, the Councils of Grey County and Owen Sound met together to try and iron out a solution. At the base of the County's objection was

Sports had long been part of Owen Sound. The 1901-02 Owen Sound Hockey
Club; top row (l-r) R.D. Bloomfield, J.N. Buddy, J. Skinner (Executive), J.S. Crate
(Executive), R.D. Murray; middle row (l-r) D.C. Morrison (Executive), R.L. Adolph
(Executive), R.T. Hamilton (Manager); J.E. Cameron (President); G.A. Ferguson
(Secretary); J. Ramsay (Executive); front row (l-r) T.J. Simons, H.H. Williams, A.R.
Grant (Captain), F. McKenzie (Mascot), D.A. Galloway, B.F. Johnston, W. Johnson.
Courtesy County of Grey-Owen Sound Museum.

payment of the newly established County road system. Unfortunately,
this joint meeting failed to produce a satisfactory agreement.

Two weeks later, Grey North MLA, D.J. Taylor, introduced a private members bill to the legislature proposing the incorporation of
Owen Sound as a city. On April 22, Taylor's bill was heard by a special committee of the legislature. At this meeting Owen Sound's
request met a stumbling block in the person of H.G. Biggs, the Minister of Public Works and Highways. The Minister told the Committee that he would oppose the bill unless a provision was made that
made Owen Sound responsible for paying a share of the construction
and maintenance of county roads which served Owen Sound.

The two sides met in Biggs' office to negotiate a settlement. After
much discussion, an agreement was ironed out. A suburban area commission was to be formed and Owen Sound and the county would

Alexandria Lacrosse Club, the C.L.A. Intermediate Champions 1908: oval shots
(l-r) H. Wilson, W.H. Smith (Vice-President), R. McClean (President), Hon. A.G.
MacKay (Hon. President), A.E. Rankin (Sec. Treasurer), C. Thompson; players
(l-r) S. Kelly, A. Patterson, T. Neving, C. Kempke, G. Thompson, J. Armstrong,
L. Jones, S. Chesney, N. Anderson, W. Patterson, R. Hare, W. Cummings, N.
Munroe, G. Bearman, F. Thompson. *Courtesy County of Grey-Owen Sound Museum.*

share equally in the cost of construction and maintenace of roads up
to a limit of $12,000 per year and the province would contribute up
to 40% of construction costs.

The Legislative committee proposed that Owen Sound would
become a city on June 1, 1920. However, there was another snag in
the plans. A circus was slated to arrive in Owen Sound on May 31 and
remain for a few days. Mayor Patterson was concerned that the
clowns, elephants and tigers would prove to be a bigger attraction to
his citizens than festivities surrounding the achievement of city status!
Consequently it was decided that the official date of Owen Sound's
becoming a city would be July 1.

The proclamation from the Lieutenant-Governor declaring Owen
Sound a city was flown to Owen Sound by a flying squadron led by
two of the Allies greatest ace pilots in World War I, Lieutenant-
Colonel William Barker, and Owen Sound's Lieutenant-Colonel W.A.
"Billy" Bishop. An Owen Sound native, Bishop had joined the Allied
Forces as a fighter pilot in the First World War. The boy from Owen
Sound was not long getting a reputation as an ace fighter pilot, shoot-

ing down dozens of German fighters in one-on-one air battles. During the afternoon of the festivities, Bishop and his squadron thrilled the hometown citizens with a daring aerial acrobatic display in the skies over Victoria Park. After the show the pilots provided flights over the new city for $10.00.[4] In the Second World War, Billy Bishop was given the rank of Air Marshall in the RCAF.

At the ceremonies the oldest citizen in the community made a presentation to the first child born in the "city." There were many other activities on that special occasion. These included a baseball game between teams from Owen Sound and Meaford, a football match between Owen Sound and Stratford, horse racing, a rowing race in the harbour and a boxing tournament featuring boxers from Toronto. A fireworks display and main street dance concluded the festivities. A large number of visitors from Port McNicoll, Victoria Harbour and Midland travelled to Owen Sound for the event aboard the CPR steamship *Alberta*.[5]

Perhaps Owen Sounders had just became comfortable about who they were and what their city had become, or perhaps they were just coming of age. During this era culture, sports and other pastimes became the mark of a community's status. The newspapers and other sources, instead of focusing primarily on industrial growth and development or economic rivalry with neighbours such as Collingwood and Wiarton, focused now on the successes and failures in the arena of sports. A victory over the Collingwood hockey team now seemed just as important as the "dredging coup" over that same community a half century earlier. It seems status symbols of that era had more to do with shooting pucks into a net as athletic prowess became an important barometer for measuring a community's success!

Cultural events and sporting events filled the leisure hours of the community. This new era brought visitors of international prestige to the community and in 1924 and 1927 the Junior Greys claimed the national championship in Canada's national sport, hockey.

One of the many internationally known intellectuals who came to enlighten the minds of the citizens of the community was the former suffragette leader Emily Pankhurst. On the occasion of her lecture at First Methodist Church, she spoke about the threat of Bolshevism and the suppressive nature of life in Soviet Russia.

On June 3, 1922 George Lynus, a famous Canadian golfer drove the first golf ball down the first fairway to open the new Owen Sound Golf

The 1924 Memorial Cup Champs: back row (l-r): Harvey Silverthorne, W.C. Young (an Owen Sound grocer), Perry Ryan, Mel "Butch" Keeling, Earl Pratt, Jimmy Jameson, Fred Elliott; middle row (l-r) Ted Graham, "Dutch" Cain, ____ Flarity; front row (l-r): Ralph "Cooney" Weiland, Hedley Smith, "Shorty" Wright. *Courtesy County of Grey-Owen Sound Museum.*

and Country Club. This event marked the culmination of more than two years of hard work and planning by many citizens of the community.[6] The course was located on property previously known as the Glen Airston Estate just south of Balmy Beach. E.C. Spereman, who later would become an Owen Sound magistrate, and a self-appointed committee including M.D. Lemon, R.P. Findlay, D.E. MacIntyre and H. Bovell had surveyed the piece of land. Other leading citizens in the community were canvassed for their opinions. After agreement had been reached, the property was purchased for $7,800 from Robert Glen.[7]

Later, on August 28, 1920 about forty people attended a meeting held in the council chambers and the committee which had purchased the property was formally elected as provisional directors and a name was selected for the golf club. A three-day stock selling campaign raised about $27,000 and by the end of the year that total had exceeded $31,000 and there were more than 230 shareholders.[8]

The first official executive[9] was elected at a shareholders' meeting in the council chambers on October 14, 1920. Nicol Thompson, the club professional at the Ancaster, Ontario, Golf and Country Club was hired to lay out the new course and the Toronto golf architect firm of Thompson, Cummings and Thompson were hired to construct the course.[10] In 1921, a temporary course was laid out for use of the 150 members and William Brazier was hired as the club's first professional and a women's advisory committee[11] was selected to help with the preparations for the official beginning of the new course.[12]

The Owen Sound Golf and Country Club received acclaim far and wide for its design and the quality of the course. In the 1950s Nick Weslock, one of the top golfers of that era, claimed that this course was "...second only to Sudbury's Idlewyld as the best nine hole course in the province"[13] of Ontario.

The sport of hockey holds an important place in most Canadian communities. Somehow the success of local teams reflects upon the community's vision of itself. In this circumstance the citizens of Owen Sound are no different than their counterparts in other Canadian towns and cities.

Consequently, March 28, 1924 is a significant date in the history of sports in Owen Sound. On that day the Owen Sound Greys won this city's first national hockey championship.

Today, hockey teams carry 18 to 20 players on their roster and may have a few more players sitting in the stands waiting to don a uniform in case of an emergency. The 1924 edition of the Owen Sound Greys overpowered their opposition winning 22 games, tying two, and losing a mere two games using only seven skaters, a goalie and a practice goalie! All but three were from the Owen Sound area. Ralph "Cooney" Weilland was from Seaforth, Fred Elliott from Clinton and Larry "Dutch" Cain, the Greys' captain came from Newmarket.

The final score from the game in Winnipeg was not flashed across a screen at the *Sun Times* office until 12:30 am. Fans crowded the street outside the newspaper office waiting for news of the game's outcome. In an era before Foster Hewitt's famous hockey radio broadcasts, or today's instantaneous reporting and coverage via television networks, this was the only way Owen Sounders could follow their team when it was playing away from home. When the results of the last game finally arrived by wire at the *Sun Times* newsroom, pandemonium broke out; 5,000 jubilant fans celebrated and two bands played.

While the fans had waited in the streets for the final outcome they had sung a chant which had been penned by a local music teacher, Mr. Dean. This Greys' battle song went as follows:

"I know where the Cup comes in 1924,
Right here to Owen Sound
Where it has never been before.
Who are the boys who won this fame?
Keeling, Dutch Cain, Teddy Graham,
Cooney, he's the centre
Of the great big fight,
Hedley, he's the goalie
In there every night..."[14]

Five days later, on April 2, Mayor William J. Christie urged all Owen Sound businesses to close from noon until 3:30 pm in order to meet the champions when they returned from Winnipeg. The *Sun Times* reported that 8,000 people lined the streets from the CNR station to City Hall.

Owen Sound has experienced other national titles but without a doubt, the 1924 Greys provided this community with its greatest moment in Canadian sports! Three years later, in 1927, the Greys once again repeated as Canadian National Junior Champions of hockey.

At the forefront of sporting activities in Owen Sound during this era was a volunteer group called the Crescent Club, formed at a meeting in December 1920. This meeting essentially consisted of the membership of two sports clubs in the community, the M.D.S. Club and the Midnight Crew. For many years, community sports teams and organizations had operated inspite of a lack of continuity of sponsorship and direction. Teams and athletes often wondered who would support their endeavours from one season to the next. Some sponsors, despite the best of intentions, lacked the expertise to promote and manage teams and leagues. Therefore, it was hoped that the merger of the two supporting groups creating the Crescent Club[15] would alleviate this problem.

In early 1921 the first executive[16] of the Crescent Club initiated sponsorship of a City League hockey team and started planning how the organization could become more seriously involved in the sporting life of the community. Before the start of the 1927 hockey season

An interior photo of the Owen Sound Auditorium Arena. When opened in October 1938, the arena featured the only artificial ice plant north of Kitchener. It was demolished in 1982 when the roof trusses were discovered to be unsafe. *Courtesy Grey County Archives.*

the Crescents assumed sponsorship of the OHA junior hockey team, the Greys. In their first season with the Greys, the junior club captured Owen Sound's second national title and the Memorial Cup.

Also in 1927, the Crescent Club, attempted to resurrect the sport of lacrosse by sponsoring a team in a league that featured teams from Southampton, Hanover and other area communities. This marked the beginning of a long lasting commitment to lacrosse by the organization. Perhaps the highlight of the Crescent Club's participation in lacrosse occured in 1950 when the Owen Sound Crescents captured the Canadian Senior Lacrosse championship.

In the same year, the Crescents entered a soccer team in the Western Football Association. In their inaugural season, the Owen Sound team captured the championship of the senior division of the league.

In the early 1920s, the Crescent Club sponsored and organized baseball leagues and teams for the youth of the community. In 1932, the organization decided to enter a team in the newly formed junior

The Owen Sound Wawanekas softball club reached the All-Ontario finals in 1929. In the back row (l-r): Bill Ray (Coach), Mid Grimoldy, Mercedes Morrison, Eileen Pembroke, Doreen Trout, Charlie Robinson (Manager); middle row (l-r): Evelyn "Pep" Arkles, Leone "Bunny" Keeling, Freda McGill, Helen Paddon, Lil Edgar; front row (l-r): Lila Robertson, Mary Ray (Mascot), Donelda "Nell" Taylor, Dorothy "Dot" Taylor. *Courtesy Leone "Bunny" (Keeling) Clark.*

division of the Grey County Baseball League. Once again the first year of operation proved successful for the Crescents as the team won the league championship.

The community's growing passion for hockey, and skating in general, led the city to the conclusion that a new arena was necessary. Although meeting the increased need for ice time was a concern, the larger reason for building a new arena was simply competition. The teams from rival cities such as Kitchener had artificial ice to practice and play on. In winters of great temperature fluctuations it was difficult for local teams to find ice. Some winters the local teams could not start playing until January!

On Wednesday, October 26, 1938 the new Owen Sound Auditorium-Arena opened amid great fanfare. The focal point of interest and attention was an artificial ice machine. Many area fans were confident that Owen Sound hockey teams would once again rule! Citizens of the area were not only proud of the teams which had so successfully represented Owen Sound in the sport, but also of the many players who had gone to establish themselves in the world of professional hockey. The day the new arena opened the *Sun Times* printed a special section featuring Owen Sound's hockey past. Also included in this segment were pictures of public school hockey teams with the title "Future Stars Learn Their Hockey in Public School." Ironically, one of the youngsters in one of the pictures is Harry Lumley, who, only a decade later would star in the National Hockey League. He is considered by many to be the greatest hockey player ever to come from Owen Sound. At the end of his NHL career, he was elected to the Hockey Hall of Fame!

The new arena was located at the corner of 2nd Avenue East and 11th Street. The site had been originally designated as Lots 5 and 6 on Water Street. Lot 6 had been purchased by Captain F.H. Smith in 1853. In 1858, a warehouse, simply known as the Smith warehouse was erected, and 80 years later it was still standing at the back of the newly constructed arena.

Lot 5 had originally been purchased from the Crown by James Sutherland. Subsequently, W.A. Geromaly of Tara had held the title. Latterly, coal and coke dealers Davis-Smith-Malone Co., owned the lot until they sold it for the arena.[17]

This arena remained the focal point of hockey in the City of Owen Sound until 1982 when it was condemned. It was replaced by a state of the art arena and community centre known as the Bayshore Community Centre which was opened on November 5, 1983. In 1995, the arena was renamed the Harry Lumley Bayshore Community Centre in honour of the Owen Sound native and outstanding goaltender.

Women were also active on the sporting scene in Owen Sound. Perhaps the most famous of these ventures into the world of sports was the Owen Sound Wawanekas[18] softball team. In 1929, these Owen Sound girls won 16 games, tied one and lost only three regular season games. Then, the catcher never wore a mask and only the catcher and first baseman wore gloves.

After winning all their play-off games, they went to Oakville to play for the Southern Ontario Women's Softball Association championship. Interest in the team was so great that 20 carloads of fans travelled to Oakville to cheer their team on to victory. October 14, 1929 marked the date of the first game of the All-Ontario Softball Championships between the Wawanekas and North Bay. Mayor Christie declared the day a holiday and encouraged the entire community to go the game and cheer the team on to victory. The Wawanekas responded. A crowd of 2,500 crammed St. George's Park. Wawanekas won the first game, 14-4, but unfortunately, lost the second game in North Bay. The third game was played in Orillia and approximately 400 Owen Sounders made their way to that town to support their team. Unfortunately, the Wawanekas lost.[19] But they remained a force in Ontario Women's Softball for many years.

It is obvious that by the 1920s, sports had become a major part of the life of the community of Owen Sound. Sports and recreation had always been of significant interest to Owen Sounders. However, in the early days prior to 1900, building and sustaining a way of life had been of paramount importance. The dawning of the twentieth century had marked the beginning of an era where leisure provided individuals with more time for activities such as the arts, sports and, perhaps, politics.

On the Social Side

By the 1890s Owen Sound's society had become more settled and affluent. The life of the pioneer struggling to eke out survival from an unforgiving environment was but a memory in the minds of the older members of the community. The increase in income and leisure hours led to interest in sports and sporting events as well as a clamour for various other forms of entertainment.

During the 1890s and well into the first three decades of the twentieth century, Owen Sound was a popular spot for the travelling theatrical troupes and stock companies which provided regular entertainment fare in the days before the movies. These groups would arrive in Owen Sound and perform before packed houses of enthusiastic fans. Of all the road shows, none were so enthusiastically welcomed as the Marks Brothers, farm boys turned theatre performers from the Christie Lake area of eastern Ontario. The five brothers, Robert W., Joe, Tom, Ernie, and Alex, each with his own individual touring troupe, performed to packed houses across Ontario and into the United States for over 50 years. Their wives and other family members played leading roles and contributed much to their success.

Annually, the community would look forward with much anticipation, to the return of live theatre. At least two Marks brothers would entertain in Owen Sound each year. One would arrive in the fall and the other would perform for a week in the spring. In the early years the admission price to a Marks Brothers performance in Owen Sound ranged from 10 cents to 20 cents to 30 cents. Later the prices increased

One of the many publicity shots of members of the Marks Brothers Theatre Troupe. Front row (l-r): May A. Bell Marks, George Marks, R. W. Marks, Gracie Marks; standing: Joe Marks, Alex Marks. May A. Bell and R. W. (oldest brother) were married and George was her son by a previous marriage. Joe, the second oldest, was married to Gracie. Alex was brother number 5. *Courtesy Perth Museum.*

to 25 cents and 35 cents. These admission prices were higher than the cost of a loaf of bread, a dozen eggs or a pound of butter but the Marks Brothers, or any other troupe for that matter, seldom played to a less than standing-room-only crowd in Owen Sound.

The women of Owen Sound have played a vital role in the development of the community. Unfortunately, the history of their varied roles is very sketchy as most of the information that has travelled down through time was written by men about men, producing a male-dominant record. It is recognized, however, that the myriad contributions made by women were essential to the growth of Owen Sound. During the early days the key public figures were all male, but without women working in the fields, raising children and performing other innumerable tasks life would have been far more difficult for all.

As the region became more developed and the working long hours seven days a week just to survive became but memory, the citizens of the area began to have leisure time. It is during this era that women began to become more visible in the public record.

One of the first women to make her "public" mark in the history of Owen Sound was Mrs. R.J. Doyle. The sister of A.M. Stephens, Mary was born in 1829 and would arrive in Owen Sound in 1851 where, at the age of twenty-two she would start a private school. She married R.J. Doyle, a successful insurance agent who also invented a cement making process.

A member of the Disciples of Christ Church, she was an ardent supporter of the temperance movement. Her disgust over the abuse of alcohol in Owen Sound led her to call a meeting in the 1870s to form an organization to promote prohibition. In May of 1874 she helped to organize the Women's Prohibition Society which ultimately became the first Women's Christian Temperance Union chapter in Canada. By the time Mary Doyle died in February 1892, she was known as the "Mother of the W.C.T.U. in Canada".

By the mid-1880s leisure time was ever-increasing, for the more prominent families and many women in the community came together to form the Angelica Shakespeare Club. One of the leaders of this organization was Annie Jaffray Eaton, the wife of Christopher Eaton, a successful Owen Sound brewer.

In 1897, under the leadership of Annie Eaton, the same group of women formed the Women's Music Club with a membership of 78 women. Until the beginning of the First World War the Club provided their own entertainment, but the membership of the Club had grown to such an extent that they were able to bring musicians from Toronto and elsewhere to perform at charity recitals and teas.

In 1905, Mrs. Eaton became the first regent of the Earl Grey Chapter of the Imperial Order of the Daughters of the Empire. During the First World War, she followed her son, Jaffray, to England. There she established and operated the "Grey Rooms" in a building owned by the Toronto Globe. She, and Mrs. Howey, the wife of Dr. Richard Howey, who had enlisted in the Medical Corps, provided the "Grey Rooms" for the use of soldiers from Grey County. The extent of the gratitude felt by the soldiers towards Mrs. Eaton was illustrated when she died in 1937. At the graveside, a firing squad fired a volley across her open grave and a bugler sounded the last Post and Reveille.[1]

After the end of the war, there was renewed interest in cultural life of the community. In March 1920, the Board of Trade announced that W. H. Taft, the former President of the United States would speak at Westside Methodist Church on the role of the League of Nations. On

Many exceptional brick homes are to be found along the tree-lined streets where the early industrial entrepreneurs and their families lived. Entertaining at home was a popular and expected event. This is the residence of John Wright, owner of the Wright Flour and Oatmeal Mills, circa late 1800s. *Courtesy County of Grey-Owen Sound Museum.*

March 20 more than 1,000 area residents filled the Church to hear Taft speak. According to the reports, Taft was enthusiastic about the City of Owen Sound and expressed a desire to visit again, in the summer time when the weather was more desirable!

Another distinguished visitor came to Owen Sound to speak to the citizens of the community. Emily Pankhurst, one of history's most vocal suffragettes arrived in the city to speak about the evils of Bolshevism.

As the century progressed, women sought additional outlets for their interests. In the late 1890s, women's hockey became a popular pastime. But the social values of the day put some limitations upon this activity. Hockey games featuring women were barred from public viewing. Only the fathers and husbands of the players were allowed into the arenas to watch the games. Teams could travel to other area communities for competitions only if chaperones travelled with the team.

By the early 1900s, the these restrictions were lifted and women's hockey became a regular spectator sport. Due to a lack of coverage by the media of the day, records are incomplete as to the success of the teams and the names of the players who participated. However, the February 17, 1993 edition of the Owen Sound *Sun Times* listed some of the women who played in 1903. They included: Edith (Frost) Strathey, Laura (Trethewey) Middlebro, Flossie (Bonham) Taylor, May Scully, Mary (Frost) Joliff, Eva (Pearce) Boddy, C. Pearson, Winnie (Lang) Gentle, Addie (Thompson) Barss and Maude (Painter) Greenfield. Interestingly, the President of the team was none other than Annie Jaffrey Eaton.

Women's hockey continued for many years up until the Second World War when it seemed to lose its attraction. Today, women's hockey and ringette are popular pastimes in Owen Sound.

Mary Esther (Miller) McGregor, wife of Reverend Donald Campbell McGregor was a contemporary of Lucy M. Montgomery and was writing during roughly the same period of time. Using the pseudonym of Marion Keith, she was best known for her many works dealing with pioneer and early rural scenes. Eventually, the couple moved to the Owen Sound area and lived along the Lake Shore Road. It was there that she wrote the books known as the Georgian Bay trilogy. The three, *A Watered Garden* (1946), *Shining Light* (1948), and *Lilacs in the Dooryard* (1952) reflect daily life in the Georgian Bay area and are best known for their fine portrayal of human nature. She died in 1961.[2]

The twentieth century brought more recognition and opportunity for women in Owen Sound, and in fact everywhere in the modern world. One of the best examples of a woman having a career and participating in all aspects of life is a woman who lived, worked and enjoyed life in Owen Sound. Her name was Mary Miller. Although she taught kindergarten in Owen Sound schools for 44 years, that is only part of this dynamic Owen Sound woman's life!

Mary Miller began her teaching career in 1906, training as a kindergarten assistant at Ryerson Public School. After completing this mandatory session she enrolled in the Toronto Normal School in 1907. The following year she began her formal career as a teacher when she accepted a position as an assistant at Ryerson Public School. After two years as an assistant she was granted her certificate as a kindergarten teacher.

During the First World War, Mary became deeply involved in the war effort. In addition to her teaching duties she worked hard as a member of the Women's Patriotic League, knitting scarves and gloves and gathering other essentials for area men serving in the armed forces. She also played in an orchestra which gave concerts to raise money to help the war effort. When the Farm Service was organized to help farmers bring in their crops, Mary jumped into this cause and travelled to the Niagara Region to pick fruit.

Mary Miller's life did not slow down after the war. She went back to spending her leisure hours at one of her favourite pastimes, tennis. She was not just an average tennis player. She captured the Women's Singles Championship for Grey County and from 1921–24 she combined with Ralph Cochrane to win the County Doubles title.

Because she was a teacher and an outstanding athlete, Mary was the logical choice for the position of head of the sports program at the newly established YWCA. She directed programs for tennis, hockey, gymnastics, bowling, hiking, handicrafts, soft ball and, as well, a social club. This was an after school position for Mary, but probably a full-time job for anyone else!

As if the energetic kindergarten teacher did not have enough to do, in 1920, she became involved in the C.G.I.T. She created sports and social events for C.G.I.T. camps and her efforts brought her recognition from C.G.I.T. groups across the province, resulting in her being named the director of camps for the region from Sarnia to Gananoque and north to New Liskeard. She held this position from 1930 until 1940.

Despite all of her leisure time activities, she still found time to fulfill her passion for teaching. Beginning in 1919 she taught kindergarten in the morning at Dufferin Public School and in the afternoon at Victoria. Later in her career she spent her afternoons teaching at Alexandria Public School.

The outbreak of World War Two brought Mary another challenge. Although she was deeply involved in the war effort, when her nephew, Tom Miller, became a prisoner of war she launched into a new project, organizing the Prisoners of War Association, Owen Sound branch. Mary worked tirelessly for this cause until peace was declared.

Mary also served as the president of the Women Teachers Association and, when she retired in 1952 after 44 years of teaching, she had only missed a total of thirty days of school over the entire span of her career.

By the time Mary Miller retired from teaching, the career opportunities for women in Owen Sound were expanding into sectors no longer viewed as exclusively for men only.

25

A TIME OF DISASTERS

The crash of the stock market at the end of the 1920s marked the beginning of an era of tough times in the Owen Sound area and throughout Canada. Although the 1930s have been regarded as one of the bleakest eras in our history, there were also some highlights and, on at least one occasion, a natural phenomenon not usually experienced in this area occurred.

The front page of the January 16, 1930 edition of the *Sun Times* trumpeted a success story about a local industry. The headline read "Big Furniture Shipment Largest Ever in Canada." Amidst great fanfare and a large crowd, a CPR train chugged out of town pulling fourteen freight cars, each with a large banner attached to its side stating that their contents were the product of the North America Bent Chair Company. The cars carried furniture for markets in every province west of Quebec. This was the largest shipment of furniture ever, to that point in time, in the commercial history of Canada. The freight cars held dining room, bedroom and kitchen furniture, as well as desks, Windsor chairs, and reed and fibre furniture.

This large shipment had created work, not only for many workers at the North American Bent Chair facility, but also many area lumbering interests had been kept busy providing raw materials to the company. Some of the furniture had been made from birch from company-owned forests in the Georgian Bay region. As well, large quantities of maple and other hardwoods had been procured from other sawmills in the area. To complete the huge consignment, the company had imported walnut, oak and gumwood from the United States.[1]

Disasters, as it has been noted, were not a new phenomenon for Owen Sound. But fires certainly were that most feared by all. A particularly devastating one led to the total destruction of the CPR Elevators on December 11, 1911, this on the very night of the completion of an old-time strenuous election. Amazingly, the steamer *Athabaska*, moored with her stern adjacent to Elevator A a scant few feet from where the fire started, was saved, even though there was no steam to move the engines. According to a later account, quick-thinking citizens early on the scene, grabbed the lines and pulled the vessel along the wharf out of immediate danger, "just in the nick of time."

The CPR wooden grain elevators with steam freighters moored along the wharf. *Courtesy Grey County Archives.*

Fire destroying the elevators at the port of Owen Sound on December 11, 1911. *Courtesy Grey County Archives.*

The fire was a heavy blow to the port of Owen Sound and a sore point with the ratepayers as the debentures on Elevator "B" still had several years to run and the CPR had already moved their terminal to Port McNicoll. It was not until 1925 that the first unit of the modern elevator would be built.

It was estimated that in the winter of 1933–34 there were 2,000 area residents receiving public relief. Two years later, in

150

late October 1935, the Owen Sound area felt a shock wave which was not related to the economic turmoil of the time. An earthquake shook up area citizens. The tremors were felt as far away as Meaford, a distance of almost 20 miles.

The 1930s may have been an era of tough economic times for most people but leisure activities still blossomed. Lacrosse, hockey, baseball and football were all popular during this decade, but golf was also growing in popularity. The Owen Sound Golf and Country Club was enjoying success and, to meet the demands of the growing number of golfers, a new golf course was planned in Amabel township, a short distance to the west of Owen Sound, about halfway between the village of Hepworth and Sauble Beach.

By 1938, area hockey teams could look forward to honing their skills in a new state of the art arena which was built for $50,000 in downtown Owen Sound. The new ice palace, which had been erected in a few months, contained the first artificial ice plant in western Ontario, north of Kitchener.

On another social front Owen Sound was entering its third decade as a "dry" community. The local option clause may have prohibited the legal availability of alcohol, but this did not mean that alcohol was unavailable to those who wished to slake their thirst after a hard day's work. Local police forces did their best to catch bootleggers, but they were not always successful. One of their more successful raids on a suspected bootlegger occurred in the early spring of 1930.

One Saturday afternoon, Police Chief Thomas Carson, along with constables McCaffrey and Reid arrived at the home of a suspected bootlegger. After producing a search warrant, the officers proceeded to search the residence. A diligent search revealed nothing out of the ordinary, however, there was something about a cedar-lined clothes closet which attracted the eye of the police. They made three attempts to solve the mystery of the seemingly innocent closet and were on the verge of leaving when, on a hunch, Constable McCaffrey went back upstairs to the closet.

This time he noticed a spot about halfway up the wall that seemed a little darker in colour than the rest of the panelling. After several minutes of examining the spot, McCaffrey went for his tools. With the aid of a large screwdriver he found a brass bolt which operated a spring on a hidden door. Further examination revealed that the door could be opened electrically by pushing a button located in the downstairs main hallway.

Once inside the hidden room, the police officers found 25 gallon cans of pure alcohol, and the equipment used to manufacture bootleg liquor, including a large mixing decanter and bottles.[2] The *Sun Times* reported that this was "the biggest 'find'" the police have ever made.

Saturday, November 21, 1936 was a dark day in the history of Owen Sound. On that day the city experienced its last major marine disaster. In the early hours of the day the Dominion Transportation Company's vessel, the *Hibou*, left the docks of Owen Sound harbour heading for Manitowaning on Manitoulin Island on her last trip of the season. After sailing for only a short time the distress signals were sounded. The vessel was listing to the starboard and the crew scampered to the life boats and ten crew men[3] made it to safety before the *Hibou* disappeared below the surface of Georgian Bay, about one mile off Squaw Point, a short distance south of the village of Leith and within sight of the docks of Owen Sound Harbour.[4]

As the 1930s came to a conclusion economic prospects seemed brighter. But there were dark storm clouds on the horizon. Before this decade of economic turmoil could pass into history the world was embroiled in a war which would impact on most families in Grey and Bruce.

For months Adolf Hitler had been stirring turmoil in Europe. British Prime Minister Neville Chamberlain had tried to negotiate some sort of understanding with the German leader. However, on that first weekend in September 1939, it became clear that some sort of action would be necessary to stop Hitler's quest for dominion over his European neighbours.

All weekend long hundreds of area residents gathered around the *Sun Times* building waiting for news. At six o'clock on Sunday morning the newspaper received a bulletin: Chamberlain had not received assurances from Hitler that he would withdraw his troops from Poland. As a consequence of this failure by the Germans to agree to British demands, the Prime Minister declared to the British House of Commons that Britain was now at war with Germany.

Shortly after the bulletin was posted in the window of the *Sun Times* office, the news of the impending war spread like wildfire throughout the city and neighbouring communities. The major topic of discussion in local restaurants and churches that Sunday morning was whether the Canadian Parliament would follow Britain with a similar declaration of war.

Until the spring of 1945, the war stood front and centre in the minds and actions of the community. Families listened attentively to each radio newscast and read every report in the newspaper hoping to hear "good" news about the war. Parents watched in anguish as messengers rode down their street carrying the message to a home, hopefully not theirs, that a loved one had been killed or was missing in action. When the fateful message was delivered, a hush fell over the neighbourhood. In the homes that the messenger had passed by there was a sigh of relief, which was quickly replaced by feelings of sadness and sorrow for the family who had received the devastating news.

Canada's entrance to the war meant significant changes in the community. Young men from all walks of life joined the armed forces to quell the Nazi threat.

"SO YOU GOT OFF AT THE WRONG STATION EH SOLDIER, WELL THERE'LL BE A TRAIN HERE NEXT WEDNESDAY GOIN' T'OTTAWA!"

Wartime cartooning came into its own during the Second World War. Bing Coughlin's creation of "Herbie" as the front-line Canadian soldier provided laughs in a world where there was much case for tears, humour that helped relieve the tension. *From* Herbie and Friends.[5]

Local industries such as Wm. Kennedy's turned their energies toward building and supplying the Allied War effort. On the home front ration cards were given out as every effort was made to help the boys on the front. Owen Sounders would open their community to the soldiers of the Polish Freedom Army which would train in the city. This was a group of Polish expatriates brought to the area and trained as a military unit with the goal of returning to Europe to free their homeland from the grip of Nazis.

The Second World War dominated the lives of local residents. Then, early in May 1945, the *Sun Times* office was once again the centre of attention in downtown Owen Sound. Within moments of the newspaper receiving the information over the Canadian Press wire that the war was over, the entire area began to celebrate.

Factory whistles and church bells were sounded. Everyone took to the streets. As soon as they were notified, principals at the local schools declared the rest of the day to be a holiday, releasing their students from classes to enable them to join in the festivities.. The streets of Owen Sound and other area communities were the scene of joyous celebrations. Union Jacks were unfurled in the business district. Impromptu parades were formed with marchers singing and shouting and car and truck horns blaring. The Nazis had been defeated and once again peace was at hand.

The end of the war was greeted with ecstasy by most Canadians. They were excited at the prospect of seeing sons, husbands and friends who had gone overseas to fight for their country. Unfortunately, there were also homes where rejoicing the end of the war was on a much lower key. These were the families and friends of the men and women who would not be coming home from the fight to preserve freedom.

The 1940s were a tumultuous decade. Although the Second World War dominated the first half of this period of time on the world front, there were many other noteworthy happenings on the local scene.

26

SUBURBAN SPRAWL AND THE BABY BOOMERS

The post-war period saw Owen Sound expand. The young men returning from war married and started families. The west side of the city grew as subdivisions were built on the west hill. A new public school, Hillcrest, was opened on 4th Avenue West at the top of 8th Street hill. The school which provided classes for Kindergarten to Grade 4 students was erected using buildings which had been used as barracks at nearby military bases. However, as the first wave of baby boomers grew older, a larger school was needed and in 1956, a new Hillcrest with classrooms for students from Kindergarten to Grade 8 was opened around the corner on 8th Street.[1]

Throughout the history of Owen Sound there are stories of conflict between the community and the centres of political and economic power. Beginning in the early 1840s, with the threat of the loss of their land due to an arbitrary decision by the government to resell property which had not been fully cleared or paid for, the subsequent visit of Reverend Ryerson and his negative report about living conditions in the pioneer settlement, the failure to have a rail connection, and on and on throughout its history, the community has had a mistrust of these centres of power. This sentiment is alive today, but in 1945 Owen Sound and Grey County got their chance for revenge!

Late in 1944, the conscription crisis was boiling over in Ottawa. Prime Minister Mackenzie King, desperate for a champion to lead the armed forces named the recently retired General A.G.L. McNaughton

W. Garfield Case. In 1944
Prime Minister Mackenzie
King called a by-election in
Grey North. Case, mayor
of Owen Sound at the
time, decided to oppose
McNaughton and won in
a landslide victory. *Courtesy
County of Grey-Owen Sound
Museum.*

to the post of Minister of Defense. However, the general needed a seat in the House of Commons. Liberal strategists looked about for a "safe" seat, which could be easily won without too much difficulty. It was decided that Grey North would be the place for McNaughton.

A by-election was called for February 5, 1945. At first it looked as if the opposition parties would not contest the by-election. However, things quickly changed when Garfield Case, the mayor of Owen Sound, and a former Liberal, decided to seek the nomination for the Conservative Party. Case campaigned hard to defeat McNaughton and he was not disappointed. The Grey North electorate, perhaps remembering previous slights, turned down the General's attempt to join the Cabinet of Mackenzie King. In one of the biggest by-election upsets in Canadian history, Garfield Case defeated McNaughton. In fact, the combined votes for the Conservative, Case, and the CCF candidate Earl Godfrey, were almost double that of McNaughton.[2]

This region took centre stage in the Canadian political arena during the famous by-election. But in the 1940s, the area's contribution of many whose skills shone brightly in the hockey arena was capturing attention, both locally and beyond. In 1940–41, the Boston Bruins captured the Stanley Cup in the first four-game sweep of the Cup in NHL history. Owen Sound's Pat McReavy scored 2 goals and 2 assists to help his Bruins capture the Cup. The Bruins coach that season was Ralph "Cooney" Weilland who had starred for the Owen Sound Greys when they captured the Memorial Cup in 1924.

In 1940–41, the Owen Sound Orphans played in the All-Ontario Intermediate Finals. Ironically, the Orphans got their name because according to Harry Lumley, the team's goalie, the team could not find a sponsor. This successful season with the Orphans would prove to be an important springboard to a professional hockey career for Harry Lumley. A little more than two years later, Owen Sound's Lumley would become the youngest regular goaltender in the history of the NHL. Lumley spent the rest of the 1940s tending goal for the Detroit

Red Wings. In 1950 he led his team to the Stanley Cup. Harry finished his career with stops in Toronto, Chicago and Boston. After he retired he was elected to the Hockey Hall of Fame.

During this time another Owen Sound goaltender was also making his mark in the world of professional hockey. Gord "Red" Henry starred for the Hershey Bears in the American Hockey League. But on January 23, 1949 he played his first game in the National Hockey League for the Boston Bruins. That night Red became only the sixth goalie in the history of the NHL to record a shutout in his first NHL game. Henry blanked Rocket Richard's Montreal Canadiens 3–0 in the Montreal Forum.

As the 1940s came to an end, a new world was evolving in North America and the Owen Sound region would experience changes in the coming decades which hitherto had seemed unfathomable to even the most imaginative minds. The 1950s began with Canada involved in yet another war. Society was undergoing dramatic changes. But one constant remained, this region was still a hotbed for hockey and in the first hockey season of that decade another national title came home to the Grey and Bruce region!

Harry Lumley or "Apple Cheeks," as he was more popularly known, played in the NHL for 15 years. In 1980 he was elected to the Hockey Hall of Fame. *Courtesy Paul White Collection.*

The Owen Sound Senior "A" Mercurys enjoyed a dream season during 1950–51. The Owen Sound hockey club battled the Stouffville Clippers for first place during most of the season. However, late in the season, the Mercs pulled away from the rest of the Big Seven Senior League to capture the league title. The Mercurys entered the play-offs hopeful of a long post-season run. Stouffville offered little opposition for the Owen Sounders in the first round, bowing out after five games. In the second round, Peterborough Petes were the victims in four games to goalie Bob Gillson and the rest of the Mercurys.

Gillson provided the all-star goaltending necessary for a hockey team to win a championship. But he was not alone in guarding the

A much earlier, but just as popular Owen Sound "Grays" in 1914–15. Ovals at top: J.J. Gilchrist (Vice-President), A. "Sandy" Grant (Manager), J.C. Telford (President); top row (l-r): B. Legate (Captain), L. Readmond (spare goal), K. Lenahan (goal), F. Foote, W. Butchart; middle row (l-r): L. McDonald, E. Pallister (right wing), Bill Hancock (Coach), E. Hicks (left wing), A. Matchett; first row (l-r): H. Pringle (mascot), T. Bell, T. Creighton (centre), T. Stead (Trainer). *Courtesy County of Grey-Owen Sound Museum.*

Owen Sound end of the ice, the Mercurys defense consisted of four veteran defensemen who made any opposing player "pay the price" if they ventured into the Mercs' end of the rink. Harry Kazarian, Art Hayward, Bun White and Bill Allum were as good as any defense core in the country. On the forward line there was a good mixture of veterans and youngsters. A trio of speedy youngsters, John Macdonald, Andy Grant and Bob Markle, formed the checking line. Veterans Tommy Burlington, Buck Forslund, Pat McReavy, Doug Gillespie, Jack Ingoldsby, Freddy Smith and Mike Buchacheski provided the leadership and scoring punch.

The Mercurys defeated the Sarnia Sailors to capture the Ontario title. Next, the Mercurys travelled to Sault Ste. Marie. Their Greyhounds won both games on their home ice and were so confident of victory that they didn't bother to bring a change clothes when they travelled to Owen Sound for what they figured would only be one game. But, Bobby Gillson and the rest of the Mercurys were not about to accommodate the wishes of the overconfident Greyhounds. Led by the veteran netminder, a determined defense and the well-balanced forward lines of the Mercurys, the Owen Sound team roared back to win all three home games and capture the series.

In the Eastern Canadian finals the Mercurys defeated the Dolbeau Castors of the Lac St. Jean area of Quebec by a margin of 3 games to 1. The Canadian finals were between Owen Sound and Fort Frances Canadians. After a hard fought six games the two teams were tied at three games each. On May 9 the seventh game was played in packed arena. For two periods Gillson and his Fort Frances' counterpart stopped everything the players fired in their direction. In the third period, McReavy, Forslund and Buchacheski scored. Late in the game Fort Francis staged a terrific attempt to comeback, but Gillson was equal to the task stopping all but one shot.

Late on May 9, 1951, the Owen Sound Mercurys claimed their first Allan Cup. The powerhouse remained at, or near the top of the senior hockey league for several more years.

As a youngster I remember walking with my grandparents around the harbour. In the 1950s Owen Sound was a busy port. The lands around the city's shoreline were dotted with industries. It seemed like every day trains chugged in and out of the two train stations located on each side of the harbour. They carried passengers to and from the area and great long trains carried the produce of area farms and businesses to markets

The Owen Sound City Hall festooned for its Centennial celebrations in 1957. A decade later this grand old building would only be a memory as it was demolished and the current city hall erected. *Courtesy County of Grey-Owen Sound Museum.*

far beyond the area. Maritime traffic also contributed to the bustling harbour of the 1950s. Many large Great Lakes vessels called in Owen Sound to drop loads of grain at the elevator and coal to fuel the industrial complex which surrounded the harbour.

In 1957, Owen Sound celebrated its centennial. It was decided that the city would hold its centennial celebrations in mid-summer form July 27 until August 3. The first day of the festivities included the beginning of a fishing derby sponsored by the Sydenham Sportsmen Association. A soccer match was held in the afternoon and in the evening a county music concert was held in the arena.

On Sunday, a regatta was held in the bay, followed by a band concert and in the evening there was a community church service. The official opening ceremonies were held on Monday, July 29, which was also called Warriors Day. There was a tribute to the city's Victoria Cross recipients and the Royal Canadian Air Force performed a fly past. The Army provided a band and the harbour hosted naval vessels standing at the ready to welcome visitors. Marilyn Bethune was crowned the Queen of the Beauty Contest and the entire city enjoyed a street dance on 1st Avenue West.

The next day was children's day. There was soap box derby and a children's parade. The local schools opened their doors for reunions of former students. In the evening barbershop quartets entertained the assembled throngs while others took in a lacrosse match. Wednesday was sports day and hundreds of competitors competed in tennis, little league baseball, softball and track and field competitions. In the evening Herb Rutherford's Orchestra provided the music for a street in the market square. The festivities continued until Saturday when an international swimming marathon was held. The celebration ended with a gigantic fire works display that evening.

The main street in 1957 decorated for the celebrations. *Courtesy County of Grey-Owen Sound Museum.*

The city had come of age. Owen Sound looked very much like any suburban North American city, but there were black clouds on the horizon. The opening of the St. Lawrence Seaway would result in less shipping traffic in the harbour. The once large fishing fleet in the harbour would disappear, a victim of the lamprey eels' assault on the lake trout. But ever resilient, Owen Sounders rebounded with the determination of their forefathers. New industries came to town, tourism became a large part of the economy and the city settled into the comforts offered by the technological explosion of the last quarter of the twentieth century.

This region progressed at what could be considered a predictable rate during its first twelve decades of existence. However, during the last four decades change has come at a pace which probably exceeded even the most prolific periods of growth and expansion in the previous era. The opening of the St. Lawrence Seaway in the late 1950s had an impact on Owen Sound's harbour. Now ships could transport their cargoes directly from the lakehead in Thunder Bay to ports around the world. This meant a reduced number of lakers calling at Owen Sound to drop their loads at the elevator to be transshipped by train or truck to Toronto and other points.

Great Lakes' freighters wintering over on the Owen Sound Harbour before the opening of the Seaway. *Courtesy Grey County Archives.*

During the 1960s, train traffic continued between Toronto and Owen Sound. Freight trains carried not only grain from the elevator, but other produce from area manufacturers and farmers. Many area residents used the "dayliner" service to travel between the two centres. However, this service declined as road transportation became more efficient and economical. The train service had provided a vital link between this region and the Toronto area for more than a century. Despite diminished rail service, some area residents always hoped that the train would once again run on a more regular basis. But in the 1990s, the final nail in the coffin of this hope occurred when the tracks were removed totally!

As this area developed, an important part of virtually all the communities in this area was the retail commercial sector, or "downtown" core. But, in the 1960s there were signals that the traditional shopping patterns for consumers were about to be disrupted. Perhaps the first harbinger of change occurred on the western city limits of Owen

Sound when the area's big "discount department" store opened. Shoppers from all over the area flocked to the Towers/Food City complex when it opened in the late 1960s.

Throughout North America there was movement towards the creation of shopping malls located, not in the city centres, but in suburban areas. Owen Sound would prove itself not to be the exception to the rule. First the Grey County Mall was built on the west side of the city. Next, the Heritage Mall was erected on the eastern border of Owen Sound.

In the 1990s, more "big box" stores appeared in the community and the shape of the commercial core of the region has dramatically changed. The last four decades have brought considerable changes to the economic face of the region. Owen Sound has seen its industrial base shift, but not disappear. In the same time frame, service and commercial interests have undergone dramatic changes and appear to have achieved a larger role in the overall economic pattern of the area.

The 1960s signalled the beginning of dramatic changes to the educational and cultural landscape of the Grey and Bruce region. The rapid growth of technology after the Second World War brought innovations which would change the way children received their education. Throughout North America, the demographic of society was changing. Cities, both large and small, experienced growth in the form of suburban sprawl. Families moved to single storey bungalows on the outskirts of towns away from the core of the communities. This factor, as well as the fact that there had been a dramatic increase in the birth rate after the war, put pressure on the existing school system.

By the late 1950s, the first wave of baby boomers was getting ready to start to high school, but it was evident that the OSCVI and other smaller area high schools could not meet the demands which the next decade would bring as more and more children of the post war era reached their teenage years. Consequently, it was decided that a new high school needed to be built. In 1960, the cornerstone was laid for West Hill Secondary School which was located on 9th Street West. When WHSS opened its doors, it signalled the beginning of a new era in education in Ontario. Smaller high schools located near Owen Sound were closed and hundreds of students began taking buses into Owen Sound to go to school.

The decision to open a regional high school was only the beginning of the dramatic changes which would sweep across the province in the

Aerial view of entrance to the Owen Sound Harbour. *Courtesy Grey County Archives.*

1960s. Since the arrival of the first settlers to Grey and Bruce, thousands of children had received their education in small, often one classroom only schools, located across the area. In the 1960s, it was decided that regional schools should be built in central areas and students could travel by bus each day. The country schools, so long an identifiable landmark of rural Ontario and often the centre of social life in rural areas were closed and sold. This education revolution did not end with the erection of WHSS and regional public schools such as Sydenham Central and Keppel Sarawak. As the first wave of baby boomers approached graduation from high school it was evident that the post secondary school system was about to come under tremendous accommodation pressures. New universities were built to attempt to stem the tide. But it was the decision to create a system of community colleges which brought about the most change.

One of these new institutions was Georgian College in Barrie. Today Georgian College has expanded to include a campus in Owen Sound. This city has a long maritime tradition. Therefore it is only fitting that Georgian's Owen Sound campus is the home to Marine Navigation and Engineering programs which provide skilled men and women to continue this country's rich maritime heritage.

Owen Sound began as a small outpost settlement in the last frontier of Southern Ontario. Through the determination and pride of its citizens it rose to become an important Great Lakes port. Using ingenuity, determination and pride it survived many circumstances that would have turned many communities into ghost towns or, at best sleepy villages. Today it is a centre for the arts, sports, and leisure activities. Whatever the new millennium holds for its future is unknown. But if the traditions of the past have any impact at all, the future will indeed be bright!

OWEN SOUND TODAY

As the city of Owen Sound enters the 21st century and a new millenium, much change is evident. The community has altered greatly since its beginnings as a small clearing in the Upper Canadian forest.

In the beginning, the core of the settlement was established around what is today the corner of 8th Street and 2nd Avenue East where the City Hall now stands. The commercial focus of the community ran along 8th Street East from the river. Today, the downtown core stretches along 2nd Avenue East with commercial venues also running up and down 8th, 9th and 10th streets from their point of intersection with 2nd Avenue. However, suburban sprawl has led to the establishment of malls and other commercial ventures establishing themselves on both the western and eastern extremities of the city. In the past decade, there has been tremendous growth on the eastern edge of Owen Sound. The new OSCVI, built across the road from the hospital on 8th Street East, occupies land adjacent to Georgian College and Sydenham Central Public School.

The real commercial growth in Owen Sound has occurred along 16th Street East. This area already contained many industrial complexes and the Heritage Mall. Now, "big box" stores have been built in the area and more are contemplated. This new emphasis on this region of Owen Sound has shifted the centre of economic activity away from the traditional downtown core.

Top: Relaxing and enjoying a view of the Owen Sound Harbour. Note the large cruise ship to the right background.
Bottom: The marina on the west side of the harbour. *Photographs by Telfer Wegg.*

The quest of the early settlers was to make Owen Sound a dominant port and industrial centre on Georgian Bay, if not the entire Great Lakes. To a large degree they were successful as at the turn of the last century the harbour was a hive of activity. Large ships were regular

167

The city of Owen Sound is an interesting blend of the past and the present, with much promise for the future. At the intersection of 10th Street East and 4th Avenue West, the four corners are symbolic of the place of worship in the lives of the people. On the southern corners are the First Baptist Church and Division Street United Church, while the northern corners are home to St. George's Anglican Church and the Pentacostal Church. Shown above: Division Street United Church and left: St. George's Anglican Church. *Photographs by Telfer Wegg.*

sights in the harbour. The industries which lined the harbour belched smoke from their blast furnaces and clang of machinery turning out products for shipment to markets around the world dominated the senses of anyone who ventured near the harbour region. One hundred years ago Owen Sound looked very much as if it were going to continue as a major industrial and port city.

However, today the port still welcomes a few Great Lakes vessels each year with some of them wintering in the harbour as well. While the railway yards are gone, they have become beautiful parkland with areas created to encourage local residents and visitors alike to take a quiet stroll along the harbour on a warm evening. Most of the industrial complexes have disappeared and those that remain await the wreckers ball. Their presence along the waterway has been replaced with a new arena, condominiums and other housing complexes. Other spaces await some form of redevelopment.

Throughout the early history of Owen Sound, the citizens of the community had a fierce determination to promote and improve their home town. In the past decades it seemed this spirit had somewhat disppeared. But in the spring of 2000 it resurfaced.

For more than a decade the Owen Sound Platers had represented the city in the Ontario Major Junior Hockey League. However, the team owners, who lived in Guelph, decided to sell the franchise at the end of the 1999–2000 hockey season. Because this junior hockey league is one of the top amateur leagues in the world, there were many groups interested in purchasing the team. Unfortunately, most of these prospective buyers wanted to move the team out of Owen Sound.

As the deadline approached, it appeared as if the franchise would be moved to Cornwall, Ontario. Despite the fact that six area business persons had offered to purchase the club and the pleadings of hockey fans, the city leaders did not seem to be able to find a way to keep the team. When it appeared that the club was on the verge of leaving, the community rallied behind the six local business persons who wanted to buy the team and raised more than $600,000 in less than three days, forcing the city into taking the necessary action to retain the franchise! Although the franchise stayed in Owen Sound, it is no longer called the Platers. Instead, the new team which will continue the hockey tradition of Owen Sound Greys, Mercurys and other teams, will be called the Attack.

Owen Sound has undergone tremendous change during its sixteen decades of existence. As the community faces a new millenium, the focus seems to be on developing tourism as a major component of its economic base. Both the rich natural heritage and the strong cultural heritage of the region[1] attract thousands of tourists each year. Originally endowed by Andrew Carnegie, the Public Library owes its existence to a grant application made by the mechanics (tradespeople) of Owen Sound, many of whom were of Scottish descent.[2] Immediately adjacent to this building is the Tom Thomson Memorial Art Gallery dedicated to the celebration of the artistic legacy of the eminent landscape artist, Tom Thomson. His distinctive approach led to his work being associated with the Group of Seven. It is noted in the history of Sydenham township that Thomson, born near Leith, used to attend Leith Presbyterian Church where it is said that when he grew bored with the sermon, he used the hymn book as a sketch pad. The world's third largest collection of Thomson works are based in this Owen Sound gallery.

The community has initiated several projects to further enhance the tourist base of the economy. Pride in local heritage is manifested through museums dedicated to Agnes Macphail, Billy Bishop and the boom days of Owen Sound as a port and railway terminus. Each one serves as a cultural centre supporting special events and providing an authentic look at Owen Sound's past.

Owen Sound today. Top: A view of 10th Street West, looking east.
Bottom: Looking north, along 2nd Avenue East. *Photographs by Telfer Wegg.*

In addition to these cultural facilities, Owen Sound boasts of its
Georgian Bay Symphony and of its internationally known Highland
Dancers. Artists of all mediums are drawn to the area. Special studio
tours, gallery exhibitions and weekly displays at the Farmers' Market
speak to their creative energy. Each summer in mid-August thousands

of music fans flock to to Kelso Beach on the west shore of Owen Sound to attend Summerfolk. This music festival attracts exceptional musicians eager to perform in a venue that has proven successful to the launching of enduring careers in the music industry.

During the last week of the summer hundreds of boats can be seen in the bay and hundreds more fishermen line the docks of the harbour, hoping to catch a trophy salmon in the Owen Sound Salmon Spectacular Fishing Derby. In all, several thousand anglers and their families come to Owen Sound each year to take part in what has become one of the major fishing derbies in Ontario.

In November of each year, the Festival of Northern Lights illuminates the streets of Owen Sound. Through the magic of lights and the enthusiasm and hard work of hundreds of volunteers, Owen Sound becomes a wonderland of Christmas lighting set up to display various themes. In recent years, the festival has become an important stop for tourists during the Christmas season.

These are but a few of the many initiatives taken by the City, private groups and individuals to promote Owen Sound as a popular tourism destination.

In 1920, Owen Sound sought to become a city and as a result separated from Grey County. In January 2001, Owen Sound will once again join the County of Grey. One of the interesting results of this reunion is another initiative which is designed to attract more tourism to the region. It is hoped that in 2002, the sesquicentennial of Grey County, a new Heritage Centre will be opened on the grounds of the current County of Grey-Owen Sound Museum.

The City of Owen Sound has a rich human and natural heritage. It was the early settlers who through determination battled to make their community a dominant Georgain Bay port and industrial centre. This same determination has helped Owen Sound weather many a storm throughout its history. With this attitude at the forefront, the future can only be bright!

NOTES

PROLOGUE

1. Croft, M.M., *Forth Entrance to Huronia*. (Owen Sound: Stan Brown Printers, 1980)19.
2. Barry, James, *Georgian Bay, the Sixth Great Lake*. (Toronto: Clarke, Irwin & Company, 1971) 57–58.

1—ABORIGINALS OF THE AREA

1. Unfortunately an intensive library of Native history for this area does not exist. For a more descriptive and detailed analysis of Native life in this area see *The History of the Saugeen Indians* by Peter Schmalz.
2. Schmalz, Peter, *The History of the Saugeen Indians*. (Ottawa: Ontario Historical Society, 1977) 4, 5.
3. Ibid, 8, 9.
4. Ibid, 61, 62.
5. Ibid.
6. White, Paul, "Natives of Bruce faced many Invaders," Owen Sound *Sun Times*, November 28, 1997.
7. Schmalz, Peter, *The History of the Saugeen Indians*, 69.

2—A CLEARING IN THE WILDERNESS

1. Guillet, E. C., *Pioneer Days in Upper Canada*. (Toronto: University of Toronto Press, 1964) 19.
2. Arran Township Historical Society, *Reflections of Arran, 1852–1982*. (Owen Sound: Stan Brown Printers, 1982) 11.
3. Ross, A.H., *Reminiscences of North Sydenham: A retrospective sketch of the villages of Leith and Annan, Grey County*, Ont. [Owen Sound: Richardson, Bond & Wright Ltd., 2nd Ed. 1991.] 179. The references to the Couture and Desjardins families.

4. Barry, *Georgian Bay: The Sixth Great Lake*. 41.
5. Berton, Pierre, *The Arctic Grail: The Quest for the North West Passage and the North Pole 1819–1909*. (Toronto: McClelland and Stewart, 1988) 193.
6. Crichton, Robert, "Impressions of Owen Sound in 1851," (Ontario Historical Society, 1920) 11.
7. Ross, *Reminiscences of North Sydenham*. 9.
8. Ibid. 38

3—JOHN TELFER, LAND AGENT

1. Thomas Rutherford was a second cousin of one of Scotland's most famous national heroes, Sir Walter Scott.
2. Ross, 208–209, and Croft, M.M., *Fourth Entrance to Huronia*. 25.
3. Stephens, A. M., *The Early Days of Owen Sound*. (Owen Sound: C. J. Pratt, Book and Job Printer, 1873) 6; Also in Davidson's *New History of Grey County*. 308.
4. Stephens, A.M., 3–6.
5. Ibid, 4, 5.
6. Ibid, 6.

4—THE *FLY*

1. Ross, *Reminisences of North Sydenham*. 50.
2. Stephens, *The Early Days of Owen Sound*. 9.
3. Ibid, 11.
4. Ibid, 13.
5. Guillet, *Pioneer Days in Upper Canada*. 73–74.
6. Ross, *Reminiscences of North Sydenham*. 41.
7. Stephens, *The Early Days of Owen Sound*. 14.
8. Ibid.
9. Ibid.
10. Ibid, 14, 15.
11. Ibid, 15.
12. Ibid.
13. Ibid.
14. Ibid, 16.
15. Davidson, *A New History of Grey County*. Owen Sound: Richardson, Bond and Wright Ltd., (1972) 310.
16. Stephens, *The Early Days of Owen Sound*. 17.
17. Ibid, 17.
18. Ibid.

5—THE IMPACT OF ISOLATION

1. Stephens, *The Early Days of Owen Sound*. 13.
2. Ibid, 18.
3. Ibid, 18, 19.
4. Ibid, 9.
5. Ibid.

6—DETERMINATION AND INNOVATION

1. Davidson, *A New History of Grey County*. 426.
2. Stephens, *The Early Days of Owen Sound*. 11.
3. White, Paul W., "Lime Kilns Began Early," Owen Sound *Sun Times*, September, 1994. When the author originally wrote in the Owen Sound *Sun Times*, about early lime kilns in the area, many readers responded with information about other kilns which had been either located on their family property or elsewhere in the region, suggesting that the lime kiln industry flourished not only in Owen Sound, but in the Grey and Bruce region in general.
4. Ross, *Reniniscences of North Sydenham*. 40.

7—THE BEGINNING OF MARITIME COMMERCE

1. Davidson, *The New History of Grey County*. 314.
2. Barry, *Georgian Bay: The Sixth Great Lake*. 98.
3. Barry, James P., *Georgian Bay: An Illustrated History*. (Erin: Boston Mills Press, 1992) 34.
4. Davidson, *A New History of Grey County*. 360.
5. Christmas, Rev. Henry (ed.), *The Emigrant Churchman in Canada*, Vol.I, (London: Richard Bentley, New Burlington Street, 1849) 210. (Author's Note: We do know that while Rose was in this area, he purchased a parcel of land which he bequested to be used for the erection of an Anglican Church. On August 8, 1881, a stone church was built on this land at the corner of Division and Hill Streets, the present-day site of St. George's Anglican Church. Two local church historians, Mark Lemon and David Tupper, discovered Rose's published account of his travels in this region and they graciously made their copy of this publication available to this author.)
6. Ibid, 214, 215.
7. Ibid, 222, 223.
8. Ibid.
9. Ibid.
10. Ibid.
11. Davidson in *A New History of Grey County* lists the launch as 1847, while James Barry in *Georgian Bay: The Sixth Great Lake* suggests that it was 1848. Perhaps they are both correct. It is possible that construction began in 1846, but was not completed until two years later, thus Barry's launch date of 1848.
12. Davidson, *A New History of Grey County*. 359.
13. Barry, *Georgian Bay: The Sixth Great Lake*. 98.
14. Ibid, 98, 99.
15. Rose, *The Emigrant Churchman in Canada*. 223.
16. Ibid.

8—FROM A WILDERNESS CLEARING TO THE TOWN OF OWEN SOUND

1. The *Times* was founded on Decembr 2, 1853. In 1918, it was amalgamated with the Owen Sound *Sun*. The Owen Sound *Sun Times* became a daily publication in 1922.
2. *Comet*, (Owen Sound) June 28, 1851.
3. Croft, *Fourth Entrance to Huronia*, 48.

4. *Comet*, March 13, 1852.
5. *Comet*, March 13, 1852.

9—RAILWAY INTRIGUE

1. McLauchlan, "Reminiscences of Owen Sound and its District," *Ontario Historical Society*, James 1920.
2. Ibid, 12.
3. *Comet*, June 25, 1852.
4. *Comet*, April 3, 1852.
5. *Comet*, January 28, 1853.
6. *Comet*, February 25, 1853.
7. *Comet*, April 8, 1853.
8. *Comet*, April 8, 1853.
9. *Comet*, April 29, 1853.
10. Ibid.

10—MARITIME COMMERCE

1. *Comet*, April 29, 1853.
2. *Comet*, July 5, 1851.
3. *Comet*, March 13,1852.
4. *Comet*, April 24, 1852.
5. *Comet*, July 2, 1852.
6. *Comet*, May 15, 1852.
7. *Comet*, May 21, 1852.
8. Ibid.
9. "Wreck of the Lily," *Comet*, September 17, 1852.
10. Ibid.
11. *Comet*, September 17, 1852.
12. *Comet*, June 10, 1853.
13. *Comet*, April 15, 1853.
14. Armitage, Andrew, *The Day the Governor General Came to Town & Other Tales*. (Cheltenham, Ontario: Boston Mills Press, 1979) 27.
15. Ibid.
16. Ihid.
17. Ibid.

11—EARLY AFRICAN-AMERICAN CITIZENS

1. Cook, John, "A Study of Blacks in Owen Sound," unpublished, in the Owen Sound Library Local History Collection.
2. Barry, James P., *Georgian Bay—An Illustrated History*. 61.
3. Croft, *Fourth Entrance to Huronia*. 92.
4. With the exception of the John "Daddy" Hall material, the information is from an interview with Paula Niall of Owen Sound, September 2000.
5. Ken Barker, "British Methodist Espiscopal," Church History column for the *Sun Times* [not dated].

12—COMING OF AGE

1. Vick, Dorothy, From Quill to Ballpoint. (Owen Sound: RBW Graphics, 1988) 54.
2. Croft, *Fourth Entrance to Huronia*. 42.
3. *Comet*, February 10, 1852.
4. Croft, *Fourth Entrance to Huronia*. 33.
5. Ibid, 58.
6. Stephens, *The Early Days of Owen Sound*. 21–22.
7. Davidson, *A New History of Grey County*. 35.
8. "And if one man's ox hurt another's, that he die: then they shall sell the live ox, and divide the money of it; and the dead ox also they shall divide." Exodus, Chapter 21, Verse 35, *The Holy Bible*, The King James Version, Thomas Nelson Inc., Nashville/Camden/New York, U.S.A., 1972.
9. Stephens, *The Early Days of Owen Sound*. 19.

13—INDUSTRIAL GROWTH

1. Davidson, *A New History of Grey County*. 35.
2. *The Daily Sun Times* (Owen Sound), June 17, 1939.
3. Despite extensive research to date, it is not yet determined if this James Frost is related to John Frost, the prominent business man or if he is a member of another Frost family, also living in Owen Sound at the time.
4. *The Daily Sun Times*, June 17, 1939.
5. Ibid.
6. Ibid.
7. Ibid.
8. *The World Book Dictionary*, Doubleday & Company, Inc., Chicago, 1987.

14—THE GROWTH OF THE HARBOUR

1. Croft, *Fourth Entrance to Huronia*. 72.
2. McCannel, Capt. James, "Shipping Out of Collingwood," *Ontario Historical Review*, 1920, 18.
3. Barry, *Georgian Bay: The Sixth Great Lake*. 119–120.
4. Ibid.
5. Croft, *Fourth Entrance to Huronia*. 72.
6. McCannel, Capt. James, "Shipping Out of Collingwood." 20.
7. Croft, *Fourth Entrance to Huronia*. 96.
8. Ibid.
9. Ibid, 99.

15—FROM "INVASION" TO CONFEDERATION TO RAILWAY FEVER

1. Croft, *Fourth Entrance to Huronia*. 102.
2. Barry, *Georgian Bay: the Sixth Great Lake*. 106.
3. Ibid, 119.
4. Croft, *Fourth Entrance to Huronia*. 104.
5. "The White Cloud Island Tragedy of 1869," *Wiarton Echo*, December 12, 1946.

6. Croft, *Fourth Entrance to Huronia*. 108.
7. Ibid.

16—THE STRENGTHENING OF CIVIC PRIDE

1. The "dummy" clock showed the same time for fifty years, 9:03.
2. Davidson, *A New History of Grey County*. 321.
3. Ibid.
4. Hay, Ellen, "Turning Back the Hands of Time," Owen Sound *Sun Times*, January 21, 1995.
5. In the early hours of February 24, 1961, fire destroyed the entire city hall complex. The $500,000 cost of the fire was more than twenty times the initial cost of the construction of Owen Sound's city hall. In 1967, the new $376,000 city hall, was officially opened.
6. White, Paul, "Blazes! Fires Were a Problem in Owen Sound," Owen Sound *Sun Times*. Date not given.
7. Davidson, *A New History of Grey County*. 323.

17—AT LAST! A LINE OF STEEL

1. *Owen Sound Advertiser*, May 6, 1871.
2. Ibid. June 19, 1873.
3. Ibid.
4. Croft, *Fourth Entrance to Huronia*. 121.
5. Ibid, 129.

18—THE "CORKSCREW" TOWN

1. This nickname for Owen Sound can be found in many newspapers, journals and other related publications starting in this era and continuing on until the turn of the twentieth century.
2. Croft, *Fourth Entrance to Huronia*. 114.
3. Spence, R.E., *Prohibition in Canada*, (Toronto: Ontario Branch of the Dominion Alliance, Toronto, 1919) 61.
4. Croft, *Fourth Entrance to Huronia*. 132.
5. Gagan, David, *A Necessity Among Us*, (Toronto: University of Toronto Press, 1990) 7–8.
6. The United States government withdrew its consulate after the CPR relocated its maritime facilities to Port McNicholl in 1912. Although its is not known for sure if the consulate remained in the same location during its tenure in Owen Sound, during its last years the consulate was located at 175 Mullholland (832 3rd. Avenue West).
7. *Owen Sound Advertiser*, June 25, 1874.
8. Armitage, Andrew, *Owen Sound: The Day the Governor General Came to Town & Other Tales*. 32.
9. Ibid.
10. Ibid.
11. Ibid. 33.

12. Ibid. 34.
13. Ibid.
14. Barry, *Georgian Bay: The Sixth Great Lake.* 118.
15. "Dammed Sydenham so Inglis Falls would be at Full Beauty for Visit of Vice-Regal Party, July 30, 1874," Owen Sound *Times*, March 18, 1950. See also Armitage, Andrew, *Owen Sound: The Day the Governor General Came to Town & Other Tales.* 9–11.

19—ENTREPRENEURIAL GOODWILL AND OPPORTUNITY

1. Hay, Ellen, "Come Enjoy a Journey Through History," Owen Sound *Sun Times*, May 16, 1996.
2. Ibid.
3. In 1925, Agnes Campbell MacPhail changed the spelling of her surname to Macphail. Terry Crowley, *Agnes MacPhail and the Politics of Equality.* Toronto: James Lorimer & Company Publishers, (1990), 3.
4. Croft, *Fourth Entrance to Huronia.* 179.
5. Ibid.
6. In 1936 part of the waterworks complex on the north side of 8th Street was converted at a cost of $8,500 into the present market building.
7. Croft, *Fourth Entrance to Huronia.* 152.
8. Ibid. 157.
9. Davidson, *A New History of Grey County.* 323.
10. Ibid.
11. Ibid.
12. Croft, *Fourth Entrance to Huronia.* 92.
13. Ibid. 157.
14. Gagan, David, *A Necessity Among Us.* 9.
15. Ibid.
16. Ibid.
17. Ibid.
18. Ibid, 10.
19. Ibid.
20. Dr. Allan Cameron, Owen Sound's Medical Health Officer; Dr. Charles Barnhart, Sarawak's Medical Health Officer; Dr. James McCullough, Chatsworth; and Dr. George Dow, former house surgeon at Toronto General Hospital.
21. Gagan, *A Necessity Among Us.* 15.
22. Ibid.
23. Ibid, 69.
24. Ibid, 66.
25. Ibid. 67.

20—RIVALRIES

1. *Wiarton Echo*, October 31, 1879.
2. Ibid, February 13, 1880.
3. Fleming, Keith, "Owen Sound and the CPR Great Lakes Fleet: The Rise of a Port, 1840–1912," *OHS*. 6–7.

4. *Owen Sound Advertiser*, April 1882.
5. Ibid, April, 1882.
6. Ibid, "Local Notes," June 1, 1882.
7. The July 13, 1882 edition of the *Advertiser* reported that members of the Town Council and Board of Trade had returned from a Toronto meeting with the Toronto Grey & Bruce Railway. They had received assurances that the proposed grain elevator would be ready for business in the spring of 1883.
8. "Local Notes," Owen Sound *Advertiser*, June 29, 1882.
9. Ibid, July 6, 1882.
10. Ibid.
11. "Editorial," Owen Sound *Advertiser*, July 13, 1882.
12. Ibid.
13. McLauchlan, James, "Reminiscences of Owen Sound and its District," *OHS*, 13.
14. Fleming, Keith, "Owen Sound and the CPR Great Lakes Fleet: The Rise of a Port, 1840–1912," *OHS*, 6.

21—THE CANADIAN PACIFIC RAILWAY

1. Fleming, Keith, "Owen Sound and CPR Great Lakes Fleet: The Rise of a Port, 1840–1912," 8–9.
2. Ibid. 9.
3. Ibid. 11.
4. Ibid.
5. Ibid. 14.
6. Ibid.
7. Ibid. 15.
8. Ibid.
9. Ibid. 16.
10. Ibid.
11. The people of Brooke (now the northwestern section of Owen Sound) were not particularly enamoured by the station that the Grand Trunk erected in their community. To make their point, the night before the arrival of the first train, a group of men painted a large rooster on the north side of the station with the words "Boyd's Hen House" written below. Excerpted from: Beattie, W.R. and H.F. Graham, "The History of Brooke," unpublished manuscript, edited by Melba Morris Croft, 1982. 1.
12. Fleming, "Owen Sound and the CPR Great Lakes Fleet: The Rise of a Port, 1840–1912." 16.
13. Owen Sound *Times*, August 28, 1894.
14. Fleming, "Owen Sound and the CPR Great Lakes Fleet: The Rise of a Port, 1840–1912."17–18.
15. Ibid. 18–20.
16. Davidson, *A New History of Grey County*. 333.
17. Fleming, "Owen Sound and the CPR Great Lakes Fleet: The Rise of a Port, 1840–1912." 21–22.
18. White, Paul, "Owen Sound had Hard Fight to get New Elevators," Owen Sound *Sun Times*, January 11, 1997.

19. Owen Sound *Sun*, February 2, 1912.
20. Fleming, "Owen Sound and the CPR Great Lakes Fleet: The Rise of a Port, 1840–1912." 25.

22—BROADENING ECONOMIC HORIZONS

1. Rudolph, Bruce, "The Polson Iron Works of Owen Sound," *Freshwater*, Volume 10, No. 1, 1995, 3.
2. Ibid, 5.
3. Davidson, *A New History of Grey County*. 367–68.
4. The first vessel was built here in the late 1840s and more recently the *Manitoulin* had been constructed in 1880 to replace the *Waubuno*. In 1882, the Great Northern Transit Company had rebuilt the *Manitoulin* two years later and re-named her the *Atlantic*. In 1883, the Simpson Company had built the *Pacific*.
5. Rudolph, "The Polson Iron Works of Owen Sound." 5.
6. Rudolph, Bruce, "Shipbuilding Period was Short But Sweet," Owen Sound *Sun Times*, Saturday, January 14, 1995.
7. Owen Sound *Sun Times*, "First Canadian-Built Steel Vessel was Launched at Owen Sound 57 Years Ago," May 4, 1946.
8. Rudolph, "Shipbuilding Period was Short But Sweet," 7, 8.
9. Owen Sound *Sun Times*, May 4, 1946.
10. For a detailed examination of the Polson Iron Works of Owen Sound see "The Polson Iron Works of Owen Sound," by Bruce Rudolph in *Freshwater*, Volume 10, No. 1, 1995.
11. The pamphlet illustrated that the 1897 property assessment for the town was $2.959693 million and that the value of the goods manufactured in the town in 1891 had totalled $1,529,564, almost four times the amount produced a decade earlier. The pamphlet also suggested that the next decade's figures would be even higher as the 32 industries located there would increase in number and profitability due to the fact that the Grand Trunk Railway provided a second line of steel to the town as well as the fact that the North American Bent Chair Company had established operations in Owen Sound.
12. The wharves on the east side included: the town dock, 450 feet long; the CPR, 1,900 feet; the CPR slip, 1,200 feet; Keenan Brothers, 400 feet; Keenan Brothers Sawmill, 100 feet. The remaining east shore wharfage included Davis and Malone; the Northern Navigation Company, the McQuarry Tanneries, Maitland and Rixon, Imperial Cement and Carney Lumber. On the west side the wharf operations included: the town dock, 625 feet; the Grand Trunk Railway, 1,000 feet; North American Bent Chair, 316 feet; two owned by John Harrison and Company of 400 and 600 feet; as well as J.R. McLauchlan, Sun Cement Company, and Grey and Bruce Cement.
13. During the fiscal year 1921–22, 274 vessels arrived in Owen Sound carrying a registered tonnage of 155,403 tons and 203 ships left port with a registered tonnage of 70,509 tons.
14. Fort William $530.66; St. Catharines $271.17; Galt $215.03; Toronto $205.80; Windsor $196.68; Hamilton $182.04; and Owen Sound at $168.77.
15. White, Paul, "In the '20s City Fared Better Than Some," Owen Sound *Sun Times*.

16. White, Paul: King's Royal Park had Short but Opulent Life," Owen Sound *Sun Times*, March 9, 1996.
17. Beattie, W.R. and H.F. Graham, "The History of Brooke," unpublished manuscript, edited by Melba Morris Croft, 1982. 1.
18. MacLeod, Rose, *Sarawak Saga*, [Owen Sound: Richardson, Bond & Wright, 1977.]
19. Beattie, W.R. & H.F. Graham, "The History of Brooke." 1.

23—THE CITY OF OWEN SOUND

1. ____, *Mer Douce*, January–March edition, 1922, 9.
2. Ibid, 12.
3. White, Paul, "Much City Optimism During the Roaring '20s," Owen Sound *Sun Times*, July 15, 1995.
4. Hartford, A.A., *Under the Elephant's Tail*, (Owen Sound: Stan Brown Printers Limited, 1992) 48.
5. Ibid.
6. "First Opened 35 Years Ago Owen Sound Golf Club is Test To Any Golfer's Skill," Owen Sound *Sun Times*, Saturday, April 27, 1957.
7. Ibid.
8. Ibid.
9. D.M. Butchart, President; M.D. Lemon, Vice-President; R.P. Findlay, Secretary; and the Directors: E.C. Spereman, J.A. Simpson, D.E. MacIntosh, J.G. Hay, E.J. Harrison, C. S. Cameron, F.H. Kilborn, R. McDowall, and John Parker.
10. "First Opened 35 Years Ago Owen Sound Golf Club is Test to Any Golfer's Skill," Owen Sound *Sun Times*, Saturday, April 27, 1957.
11. This group included Mrs. Bovell, Mrs. G.S. Kilborn, Mrs. John Parker, Mrs. A.B. Rutherford, Mrs. C.S. Cameron and Mrs. A.B. Hay.
12. "First Opened 35 Years Ago Owen Sound Golf Club is Test to Any Golfer's Skill," Owen Sound *Sun Times*, Saturday, April 27, 1957.
13. Waugh, Dick, Owen Sound *Sun Times*, April 27, 1957.
14. Hartford, A.A., *Under the Elephant's Tail*. 57.
15. At first the club was called the Scenery City Athletic Club, however the name was soon changed to the Crescent Club which had been the name of the teams which the M.D.S. group had sponsored.
16. President R.E. "Bob" Wilson, Vice-President G.C. Thompson, Secretary-Treasurer Earl "Wash" Williams, Sports Committee: Leslie "Son" MacDonald, C.S. "Earl" Pratt, Tom "Butter" Young, Floyd McDonald and Arthur "Bud" Kreutzweiser.
17. *The Daily Sun Times*, Owen Sound, Tuesday, October 25, 1938.
18. The members of the Wawanekas were: Helen Paddon, pitcher; Doreen Trout, catcher; Leone Keeling, first base; Freda McGill, second base; Evelyn Arkles, shortstop; Lil Edgar, third base; with Mid Grimoldy, Donelda Taylor and Eileen Pembroke in the outfield. The substitutes were Mercedes Morrison, Lila Patterson and Dorothy Taylor.
19. White, Paul, "Wawanekas Walloped Foes," Owen Sound *Sun Times*, November 16, 1996.

24—ON THE SOCIAL SIDE

1. Clarke, Sharon (ed.), *Eminent Women of Grey County*. [Owen Sound: Richardson, Bond & Wright, 1977.] 34–36.
2. Background taken from *From Quill to Ballpoint 1591–1988* by Dorothy Vick published by R.B.W. Graphics of Owen Sound, 1988. p. 171–172.

25—A TIME OF DISASTERS

1. "Big Furniture Shipment Largest Ever in Canada," Owen Sound *Sun Times*, January 16, 1930.
2. Owen Sound *Sun Times*, March 3, 1930.
3. Those who survived included James Agnew, Howard Allen, Duncan Smart, Orville Parr, F. Record, E. Carr, D. McIntosh, Ross Galbraith, Ernest Rouse and Dan Rouse. Those who lost their lives included Captain Norman McKay, J. Reynolds, M. McIvor, Chester Dunham, R. Earls, James Minard and Miss Iona Johnson.
4. "Seven Die as Hibou Lost off Squaw Point," Owen Sound *Sun Times*, November 21, 1936.
5. Cartoon used with permission of publisher from Barry L. Rowland, *Herbie and Friends: Cartoons in Wartime*. Toronto: Natural Heritage/Natural History Inc., 1990, 96.

26—SUBURBAN SPRAWL AND BABY BOOMERS

1. In the 1960s, responding to the fact that the baby boomers had become teenagers, West Hill Secondary School was built on 9th Avenue West.
2. Case—7,333; Godfrey—3,118; McNaughton—6,097. In Owen Sound, the numbers were: Case—3,088; Godfrey—1,919; and McNaughton—2,604.

27—OWEN SOUND TODAY

1. Much of the information on the cultural facilities of Owen Sound of today was provided through Owen Sound Tourism.
2. Information from Lucille (Thomson) Campey who grew up in Owen Sound in the 1940s. Her father, a Civil Engineer who worked for the Ontario Department of Highways, encouraged her to read books. The library was right across the street from their home.

SELECTED BIBLIOGRAPHY

Armitage, Andrew, *The Day the Governor General Came to Town and Other Tales*. Cheltenham, Ont.: Boston Mills Press, 1979.

Barry, James, *Georgian Bay, the Sixth Great Lake*. Toronto: Clarke, Irwin and Company, 1971.

Cathcart, Ruth, *How Firm a Foundation: The Historic Houses of Grey County*: Owen Sound: The Red House Press, 1996.

Clarke, Sharon (ed.), *Eminent Women of Grey County*. Owen Sound: Richardson, Bond & Wright, 1977.

Croft, M.M., *Fourth Entrance to Huronia*. Owen Sound: Stan Brown Printers, 1980.

Davidson, T. Arthur, *A New History of the County of Grey*. Owen Sound: Richardson, Bond and Wright Ltd., 1972.

Guillet, E.C., *Pioneer Days in Upper Canada*. Toronto: University of Toronto Press, 1964.

Hartford, A.A., *Under the Elephant's Tail*, Owen Sound: Stan Brown Printers Limited, 1992.

MacLeod, Rose, *Sarawak Saga*. Owen Sound: Richardson, Bond and Wright, 1973.

McGillvary, Marion (ed.) (Arran Township Historical Society), *Reflections of Arran, 1852-1982*. Owen Sound: Stan Brown Printers, 1982.

Ross, A.H., *Reminiscences of North Sydenham: A Retrospective Sketch of the Villages of Leith and Annan, Grey County, Ont*. Owen Sound: Richardson, Bond and Wright Ltd. 2nd ed. 1991.

Schmaltz, Peter, *The History of the Saugeen Indians*. Ottawa: Ontario Historical Society, 1977.

Stephens, A.M., *The Early Days of Owen Sound*. Owen Sound: C.J. Pratt, Book and Job Printer, 1873. (Available through the Owen Sound-North Grey Union Public Library.)

Vick, Dorothy, *From Quill to Ballpoint, 1591–1988*. Owen Sound: RBW Graphics, 1988.

INDEX

INDEX

INDEX

INDEX

INDEX

About the Author

Photograph by James Masters

Paul White was born and raised in Owen Sound. After attending Hillcrest Public School and West Hill Secondary School, Paul graduated from Trent University where he majored in Canadian History and Canadian Studies.

Paul has published over 300 articles about the history of Owen Sound and the Grey and Bruce region in the Owen Sound *Sun Times.* He has also written two books about this region: *The Hockey Scrapbook; the history of the sport in Owen Sound and Bruce County regions* for the Bruce County Museum and *The Maritime History of Georgian Bay* which he co-authored with Larry Turner for Parks Canada.

Paul is currently employed as the Archivist for the Grey County Archives. He and his wife Judy live in the Township of Sarawak.

LaVergne, TN USA
14 December 2009
167028LV00004B/30/P